THE BAKER ILLUSTRATED *GUIDE TO THE* BIBLE

THE BAKER ILLUSTRATED *GUIDE TO THE* BIBLE

A BOOK-BY-BOOK COMPANION

J. DANIEL HAYS *and* J. SCOTT DUVALL

Published by Baker Books
a division of Baker Publishing Group
P.O. Box 6287, Grand Rapids, MI 49516-6287
www.bakerbooks.com

Printed in the United States of America

Library of Congress Cataloging-in-Publication Data
Names: Hays, J. Daniel, 1953– author.
Title: The Baker illustrated guide to the Bible : a book-by-book companion / J. Daniel Hays and J. Scott Duvall.
Description: Grand Rapids : Baker Books, 2016.
Identifiers: LCCN 2016009709 | ISBN 9780801015458 (pbk.)
Subjects: LCSH: Bible—Introductions.
Classification: LCC BS475.3 .H39 2016 | DDC 220.6/1—dc23
LC record available at https://lccn.loc.gov/2016009709

Interior design by William Overbeeke

16 17 18 19 20 21 22 7 6 5 4 3 2 1

Contents

What Is the Bible About?

Everyone has a story to live by. For Christians, two questions arise regarding this story: "Which story tells the true story about God, our world, and life?" and "Does my story line up with the true story?" What constitutes a basic story line is much the same in novels, TV shows, movies, and plays. Typically, the story opens with things going well. The characters are introduced, and we are given essential background information. Everything is good (or at least stable) at the start, but then a problem or crisis threatens the characters and their future. Much of the story is taken up with solving this problem (conflict resolution). Usually, during this period of resolution, the tension builds to a critical point (the climax), and the heart of the problem is solved. Finally (though this may take awhile), the resolution is worked out so that things are not just good but great. When there is no happy ending, the story is called a tragedy. The phases of a grand story are summarized as follows:

- Opening—setting provided and characters introduced
- Problem—conflict threatens the well-being of the characters
- Resolution—solving the problem
- Climax within resolution phase—most intense conflict followed by solution to heart of problem
- Closing—resolution worked out for the characters

The Bible claims to be God's story for the whole world. In the Bible we find the one grand story that best explains reality:

- Opening—Genesis 1–2
- Problem—Genesis 3–11
- Resolution—Genesis 12–Revelation 18
- Climax within resolution phase—life, death, and resurrection of Jesus Christ
- Closing—Revelation 19–22

To put the grand story of the Bible into a memorable format, consider the outline below, which uses the *k* sound:

Creation—The story begins with the creation of the world and human beings (Gen. 1–2).

Crisis—When tempted by Satan, humans choose to satisfy self and rebel (or sin) against God. Sin brings disastrous and deadly consequences: pain, suffering, death, and separation from God (Gen. 3–11).

Covenant—God begins to solve the sin problem by choosing Abraham and establishing a covenant with him so that he might become the father of a people who will worship God. God wants to make Abraham into a great nation and use this one nation to bring the rest of the world into a relationship with himself (Gen. 12, 15, 17).

Calling out—Genesis tells the story of the patriarchs: Abraham, Isaac, Jacob (Israel), and Joseph. Through a series of events the patriarchs move to Egypt, and their small group grows into a nation, but they become enslaved. God uses Moses to deliver his people from slavery through the exodus event. God's miraculous deliverance of his people from bondage in Egypt becomes a pattern that foreshadows God's ultimate deliverance of his people from spiritual slavery.

Commandments—After God rescues his people, God enters into a covenant with them (the Mosaic covenant). He gives them the law (summed up in the Ten Commandments) and calls his people to holiness. God's expectations for his covenant people are spelled out in the book of Deuteronomy.

Conquest—God uses Joshua to help his people take the promised land (Canaan).

Kingdom—God's people acquire a king. Samuel becomes the link between the judges and the kings of Israel. The first king is Saul, followed by David and Solomon.

Kingdom divided—After Solomon, a civil war leads to the division of the kingdom: Israel = northern kingdom, Judah = southern kingdom. There are many kings; some are good but most are bad.

Captivity—Because God's people have failed to worship him alone, they face terrible judgment, including the loss of the promised land. Their enemies take them captive. Israel is conquered by the Assyrians in 722 BC, while Judah is conquered and taken captive by the Babylonians around 586 BC.

Coming home—The people finally return from exile under Zerubbabel, Ezra, and Nehemiah (538–430 BC).

Christ (climax to the story)—About four hundred years later God sends his Son, Jesus the Christ, to save his people from their sins. Jesus announces the coming of God's kingdom through his teachings and miracles. His death and resurrection form the climax to the biblical story.

Church—Those who accept Jesus become part of the church—the people of God—comprised of both Jews and Gentiles. God continues to use his people to extend his offer of salvation to a sinful world.

Consummation—God closes history with a final victory over evil. Those who have rejected God will suffer judgment while those who have accepted him will live with him in a new heaven and new earth. God's promises are now fulfilled (see Rev. 19–22 and esp. 21:1–4).

The Bible is a collection of sixty-six books, but it also functions like a single book. The Bible's great story answers the basic questions of life better than any other story because it's true. We can count on it. When a person comes to faith in Christ, he or she is basically saying, "I want God's story to become my story." That's what conversion is—embracing the great story of Scripture as our personal story.

How Is the Bible Organized?

The English word "bible" comes from the Greek word for books or scrolls: *biblia* (plural). In 2 Timothy 4:13, Paul asks Timothy to bring his "books" (*biblia*) when he comes to visit him in prison. Our word "Bible" is singular because it refers to the entire collection of sixty-six books: thirty-nine in the Old Testament (books about God's relationship with Israel) and twenty-seven in the New Testament (books about Jesus and the early church). Grouping the books as follows helps understand how they are arranged and what they contain.

Pentateuch	Historical Books	Psalms	Wisdom Books	Prophets
Genesis	Joshua	Psalms	Job	Isaiah
Exodus	Judges		Proverbs	Jeremiah
Leviticus	Ruth		Ecclesiastes	Lamentations
Numbers	1–2 Samuel		Song of Songs	Ezekiel
Deuteronomy	1–2 Kings			Daniel
	1–2 Chronicles			*Minor Prophets:*
	Ezra			Hosea
	Nehemiah			Joel
	Esther			Amos
				Obadiah
				Jonah
				Micah
				Nahum
				Habakkuk
				Zephaniah
				Haggai
				Zechariah
				Malachi

Gospels	Acts	Letters of Paul	General Letters	Revelation
Matthew	Acts	Romans	Hebrews	Revelation
Mark		1–2 Corinthians	James	
Luke		Galatians	1–2 Peter	
John		Ephesians	1–3 John	
		Philippians	Jude	
		Colossians		
		1–2 Thessalonians		
		1–2 Timothy		
		Titus		
		Philemon		

The word "testament" comes from the word *testamentum,* the Latin translation of the Hebrew and Greek words for "covenant." The English word "testament" refers to a covenant. Christians accept both the Old Testament and the New Testament, while Jews who reject Jesus as Messiah reject the new covenant or testament. In the biblical sense, a covenant refers to what God has done to establish a relationship with human beings. Over time, the term "testament" came to refer to the writings that describe the covenant.

The Old Testament

An Overview

The Old Testament is divided into five parts: the Pentateuch, the Historical books, the Psalms, the Wisdom books, and the Prophets.

The Pentateuch

The first five books of the Bible (Genesis, Exodus, Leviticus, Numbers, and Deuteronomy) are often referred to as the "Pentateuch" (the "five scrolls" or five-scroll collection). In the Hebrew Scriptures, these books are referred to as the "Torah," meaning the "teaching" or "instruction." These books tell the story of God's creation of the world, of human sin and rebellion against God, of God's covenant with Abraham, of God's deliverance of his people from slavery in Egypt, of God's covenant with Moses, of God's laws for his people, and of his peoples' journey to the promised land. The last book, Deuteronomy, spells out the blessings and penalties for keeping or rejecting the Mosaic covenant.

A modern Hebrew Bible scroll

The Historical Books

The Old Testament books from Joshua through Esther are known as the "Historical books." The first group of books (Joshua through 2 Kings) is closely connected to the book of Deuteronomy and continues the story of the Pentateuch. In essence, Deuteronomy closes by posing an important question, "Will Israel be faithful to the Lord and his laws (the Mosaic covenant)?" The tragic answer is no, they will not remain faithful, and 2 Kings ends with the destruction of Jerusalem and the exile of Israel from the promised land. The second group of Historical books (1 Chronicles through Esther) is written from a different perspective. These books focus on those who have returned to the land after the exile, encouraging them to remain faithful to the Lord.

The Psalms

The book of Psalms is unique and cannot be placed in any of the other Old Testament categories. It stands alone as a book of songs of praise, testimony, and lament. The Psalms were (and are) used both in public worship and private meditation.

The Wisdom Books

The Wisdom books (Job, Proverbs, Ecclesiastes, and Song of Songs) remind God's people of the importance of listening, thinking, considering, and reflecting. Their purpose is to encourage the development of both godly character and the ability to make wise decisions in a variety of circumstances. Proverbs presents basic principles of life—things that are normally or usually true—while the other three books treat exceptions to these rules: Job (when the righteous suffer), Ecclesiastes (when a rational approach to life doesn't provide all the answers), and Song of Songs (concerning the "irrationality" of romantic love).

The Prophets

After entering the promised land, Israel turns a deaf ear to God's instructions and follows other gods. As the nation spirals downward, God sends the prophets with a final message for his people: (1) you have broken the Mosaic covenant through idolatry, social injustice, and religious ritualism, and you need to turn back to a true worship of God; (2) if you fail to repent, then you will face judgment; and (3) there is still hope beyond judgment for you—a glorious, future restoration for God's people and for the nations. This standard prophetic message is repeated throughout the Prophets. But people continue to rebel and face judgment, which comes in the form of two invasions: the Assyrians in 722 BC to destroy the northern kingdom of Israel and the Babylonians in 587/586 BC to destroy the southern kingdom of Judah and the city of Jerusalem. The prophets also promise a time of future restoration, including a new covenant that will involve all the nations of the world. This fulfills God's original promise to Abraham in Genesis 12:3.

The exact location of Mount Sinai is unknown. There are numerous mountain peaks in the Sinai desert that could be the mountain on which God appeared to Moses and Israel. Shown in this picture is a peak called Jebel Musa ("mountain of Moses"), which some believe is Mount Sinai.

Old Testament Time Line

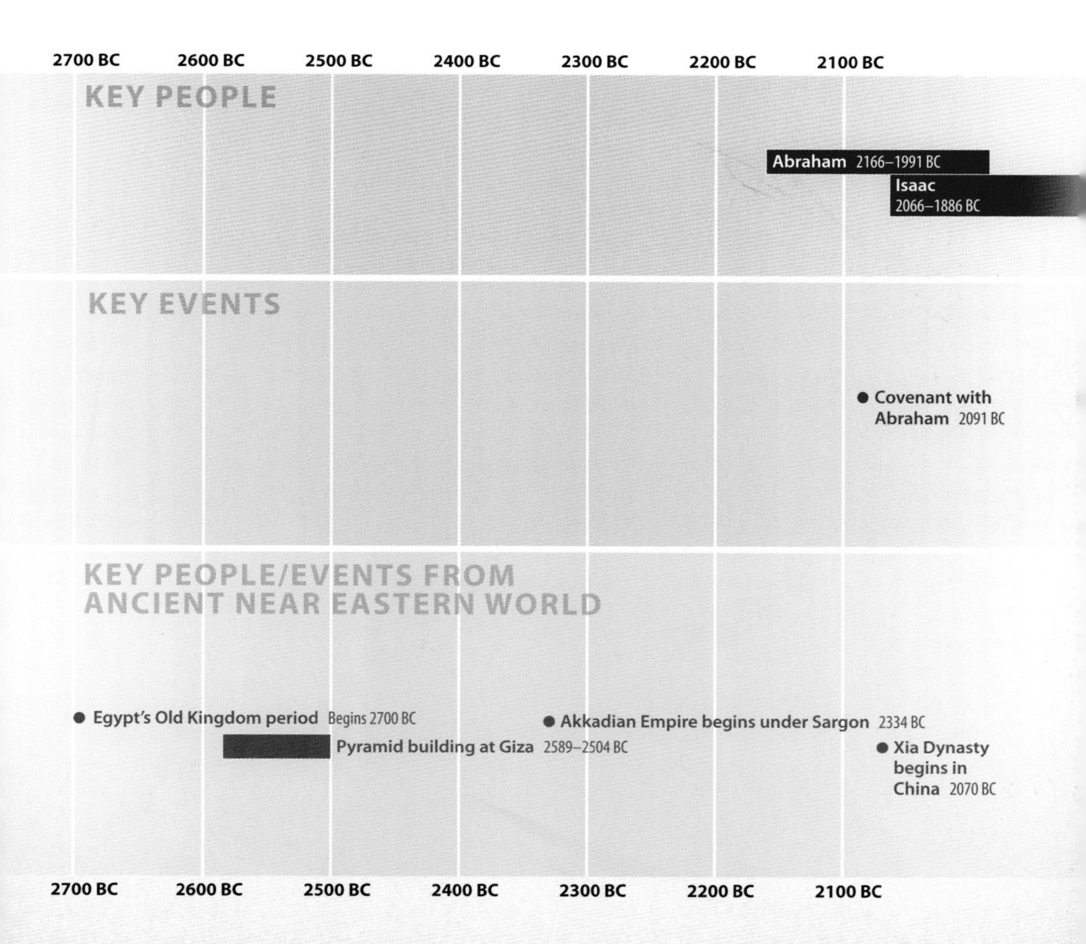

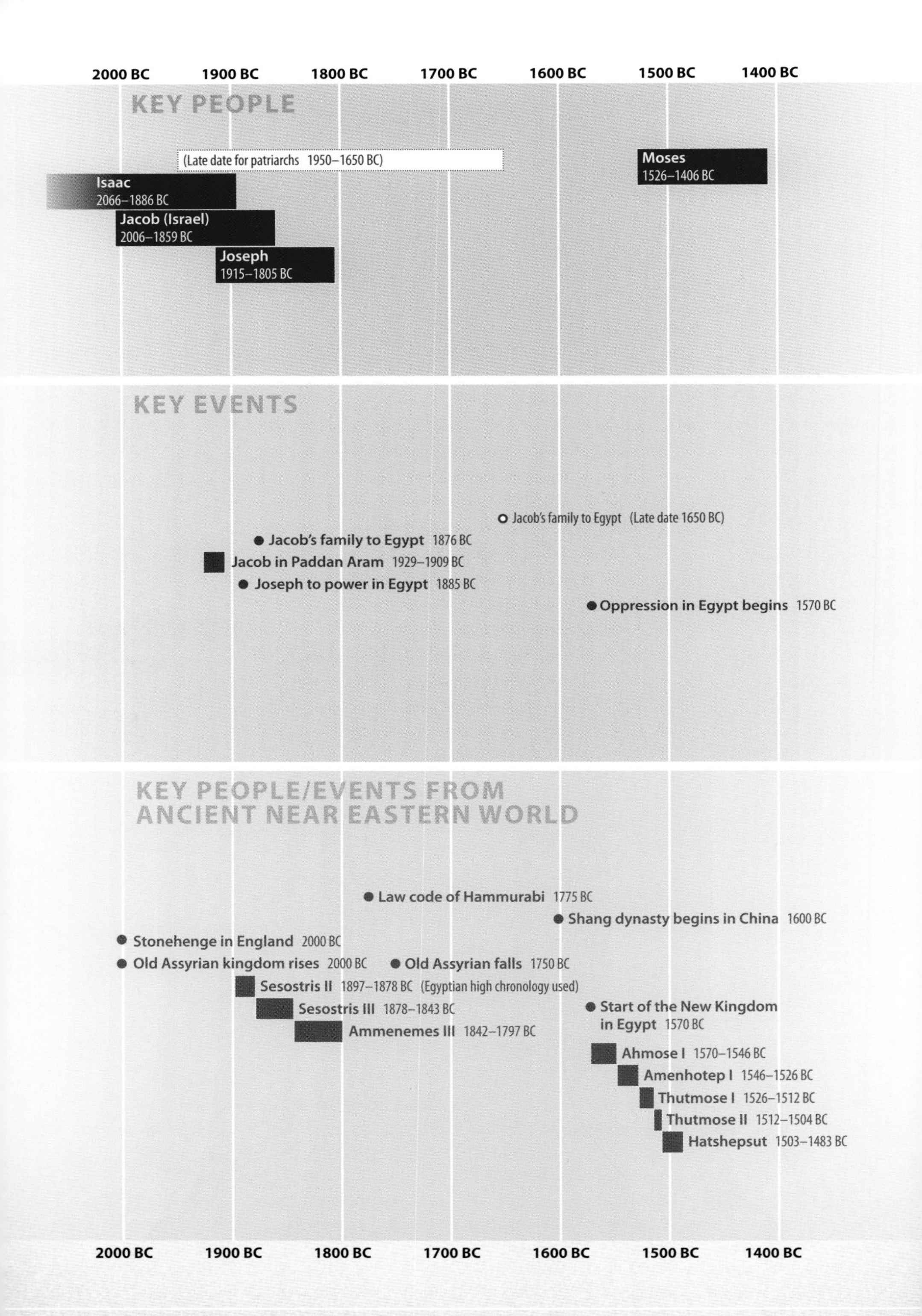
2000 BC
1900 BC
1800 BC
1700 BC
1600 BC
1500 BC
1400 BC
KEY PEOPLE
(Late date for patriarchs 1950–1650 BC)
Moses
1526–1406 BC
Isaac
2066–1886 BC
Jacob (Israel)
2006–1859 BC
Joseph
1915–1805 BC
KEY EVENTS
Jacob's family to Egypt (Late date 1650 BC)
Jacob's family to Egypt 1876 BC
Jacob in Paddan Aram 1929–1909 BC
Joseph to power in Egypt 1885 BC
Oppression in Egypt begins 1570 BC
KEY PEOPLE/EVENTS FROM
ANCIENT NEAR EASTERN WORLD
Law code of Hammurabi 1775 BC
Shang dynasty begins in China 1600 BC
Stonehenge in England 2000 BC
Old Assyrian kingdom rises 2000 BC
Old Assyrian falls 1750 BC
Sesostris II 1897–1878 BC (Egyptian high chronology used)
Sesostris III 1878–1843 BC
Start of the New Kingdom
in Egypt 1570 BC
Ammenemes III 1842–1797 BC
Ahmose I 1570–1546 BC
Amenhotep I 1546–1526 BC
Thutmose I 1526–1512 BC
Thutmose II 1512–1504 BC
Hatshepsut 1503–1483 BC
2000 BC
1900 BC
1800 BC
1700 BC
1600 BC
1500 BC
1400 BC

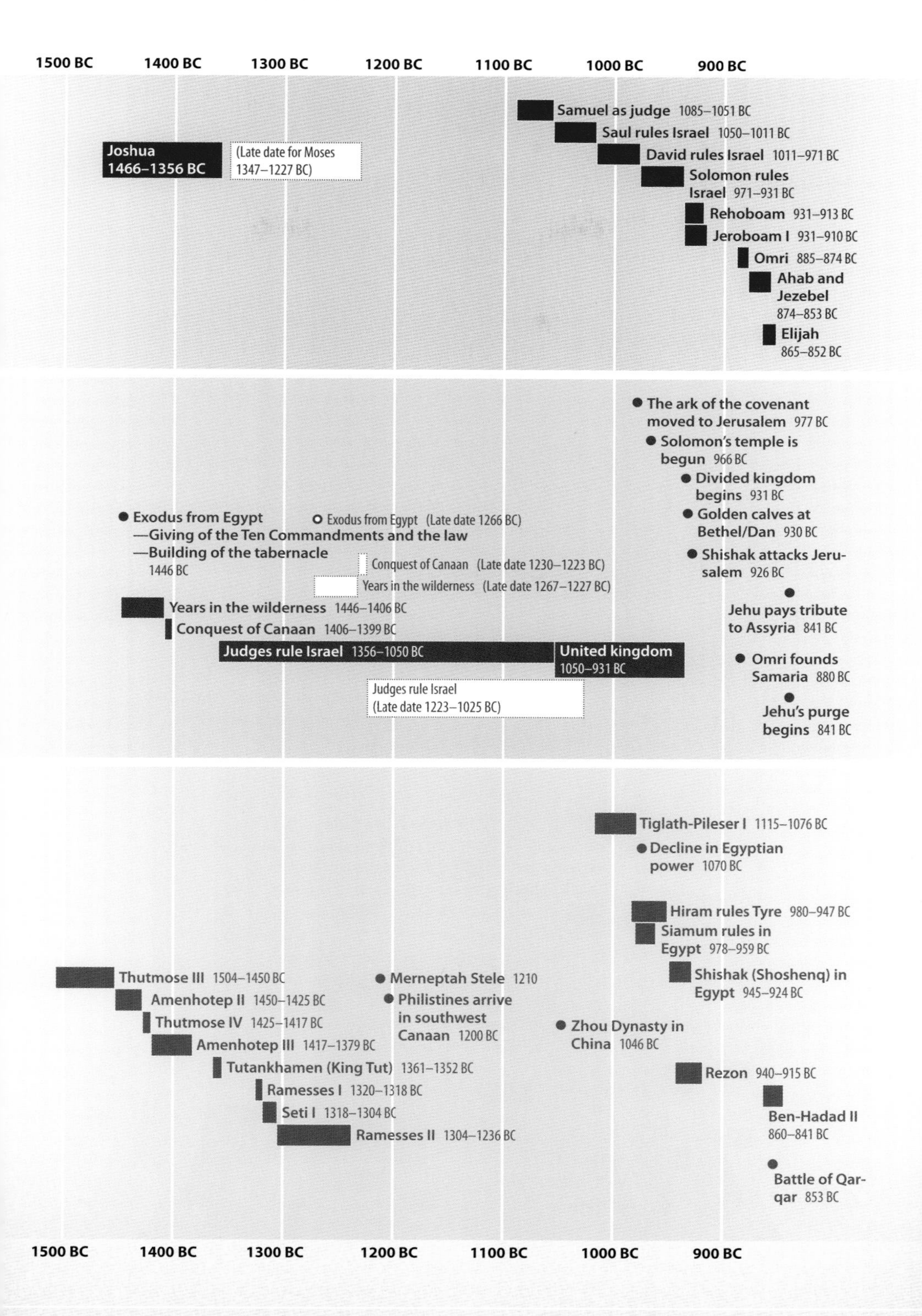
1500 BC
1400 BC
1300 BC
1200 BC
1100 BC
1000 BC
900 BC
Samuel as judge 1085–1051 BC
Saul rules Israel 1050–1011 BC
Joshua 1466–1356 BC
(Late date for Moses 1347–1227 BC)
David rules Israel 1011–971 BC
Solomon rules Israel 971–931 BC
Rehoboam 931–913 BC
Jeroboam I 931–910 BC
Omri 885–874 BC
Ahab and Jezebel 874–853 BC
Elijah 865–852 BC
The ark of the covenant moved to Jerusalem 977 BC
Solomon's temple is begun 966 BC
Divided kingdom begins 931 BC
Exodus from Egypt —Giving of the Ten Commandments and the law —Building of the tabernacle 1446 BC
Exodus from Egypt (Late date 1266 BC)
Golden calves at Bethel/Dan 930 BC
Shishak attacks Jerusalem 926 BC
Conquest of Canaan (Late date 1230–1223 BC)
Years in the wilderness (Late date 1267–1227 BC)
Years in the wilderness 1446–1406 BC
Jehu pays tribute to Assyria 841 BC
Conquest of Canaan 1406–1399 BC
Judges rule Israel 1356–1050 BC
United kingdom 1050–931 BC
Omri founds Samaria 880 BC
Judges rule Israel (Late date 1223–1025 BC)
Jehu's purge begins 841 BC
Tiglath-Pileser I 1115–1076 BC
Decline in Egyptian power 1070 BC
Hiram rules Tyre 980–947 BC
Siamum rules in Egypt 978–959 BC
Thutmose III 1504–1450 BC
Merneptah Stele 1210
Shishak (Shoshenq) in Egypt 945–924 BC
Amenhotep II 1450–1425 BC
Philistines arrive in southwest Canaan 1200 BC
Thutmose IV 1425–1417 BC
Zhou Dynasty in China 1046 BC
Amenhotep III 1417–1379 BC
Tutankhamen (King Tut) 1361–1352 BC
Rezon 940–915 BC
Ramesses I 1320–1318 BC
Seti I 1318–1304 BC
Ben-Hadad II 860–841 BC
Ramesses II 1304–1236 BC
Battle of Qarqar 853 BC
1500 BC
1400 BC
1300 BC
1200 BC
1100 BC
1000 BC
900 BC

800 BC
700 BC
600 BC
500 BC
400 BC
300 BC
200 BC
KEY PEOPLE
Jeroboam II 793–753 BC
Ahaz 735–716 BC
Hoshea 732–722 BC
Hezekiah 716–687 BC
Josiah 641–609 BC
Zedekiah 597–586 BC
Elisha 852–790 BC
Jehu 841–814 BC
Joash 835–796 BC
KEY EVENTS
Destruction of Jerusalem and the temple 586 BC
Third deportation to Babylon 586 BC
Temple reconstruction begins 536 BC
Temple reconstruction halted 530–520 BC
Temple dedication 516 BC
Second return from the Babylonian exile led by Ezra 458 BC
Hezekiah's reforms begin 705 BC
Assyria attacks Jerusalem 701 BC
Third return from the Babylonian exile led by Nehemiah 445 BC
Josiah's reforms 623 BC
Josiah dies at Megiddo 609 BC
First return from the Babylonian exile led by Zerubbabel 538 BC
First deportation to Babylon 605 BC
Second deportation to Babylon 597 BC
First Assyrian deportation 732 BC
Jerusalem's walls rebuilt 445 BC
Samaria falls to Assyria 722 BC
Esther becomes queen in Persia 478 BC
Second Assyrian deportation 722 BC
KEY PEOPLE/EVENTS FROM ANCIENT NEAR EASTERN WORLD
Babylon falls to Persia 539 BC
Sennacherib 705–681 BC
Xerxes I (Ahasuerus) 486–465 BC
Founding of Rome 753 BC
Cyrus the Great 559–530 BC
Esarhaddon 681–669 BC
Battle of Marathon 490 BC
Ashurbanipal 668–633 BC
Artaxerxes I 465–424 BC
Thebes falls to Assyria 663 BC
Gauls attack Rome 390 BC
Rise of the Neo-Babylonian Empire 625 BC
Rise of Neo-Assyrian Empire 744 BC
Herodotus 485–425 BC
Nabopolassar 625–605 BC
Plato 428–348 BC
Shalmaneser III 858–824 BC
Nineveh falls to Babylonians and Medes 612 BC
Hazael 841–806 BC
Haran falls to the Babylonians 610 BC
Ben-Hadad III 806–770 BC
Cambyses 530–522 BC
Rezin 750–732 BC
Nebuchadnezzar 605–562 BC
Evil-Merodach 562–560 BC
Aristotle 384–322 BC
Adad-Nirari III 810–782 BC
Assyria falls to Babylon at Carchemish 605 BC
Tiglath-Pileser III 744–727 BC
Roman republic established 509 BC
Damascus falls to Assyria 732 BC
Socrates 470–399 BC
Shalmaneser V 727–722 BC
Darius I 522–486 BC
Sargon II 721–705 BC
Nabonidus 556–539 BC
800 BC
700 BC
600 BC
500 BC
400 BC
300 BC
200 BC

Old Testament Maps

The Travels of Abraham

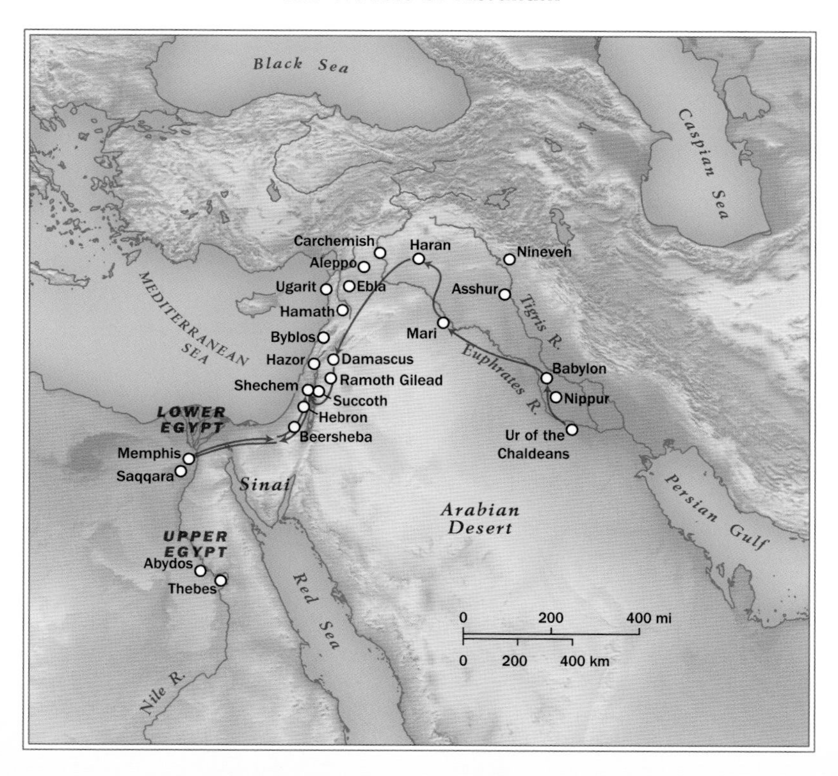

The Tribal Distribution of the Promised Land

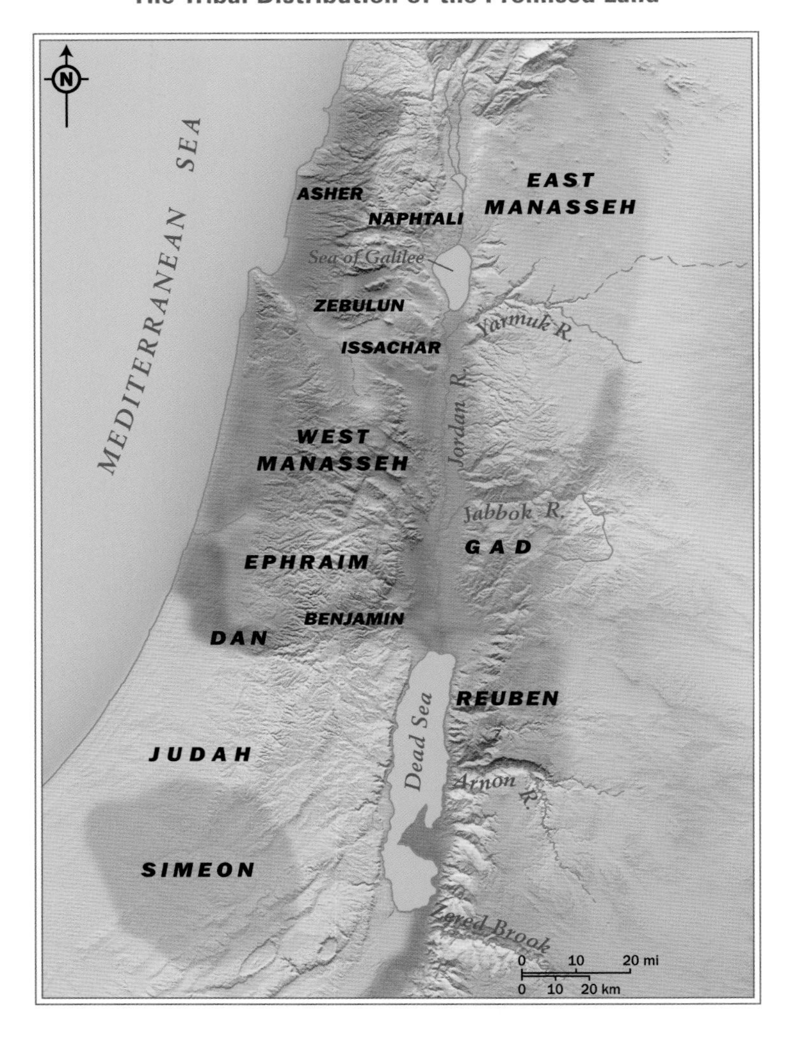

The Divided Kingdom

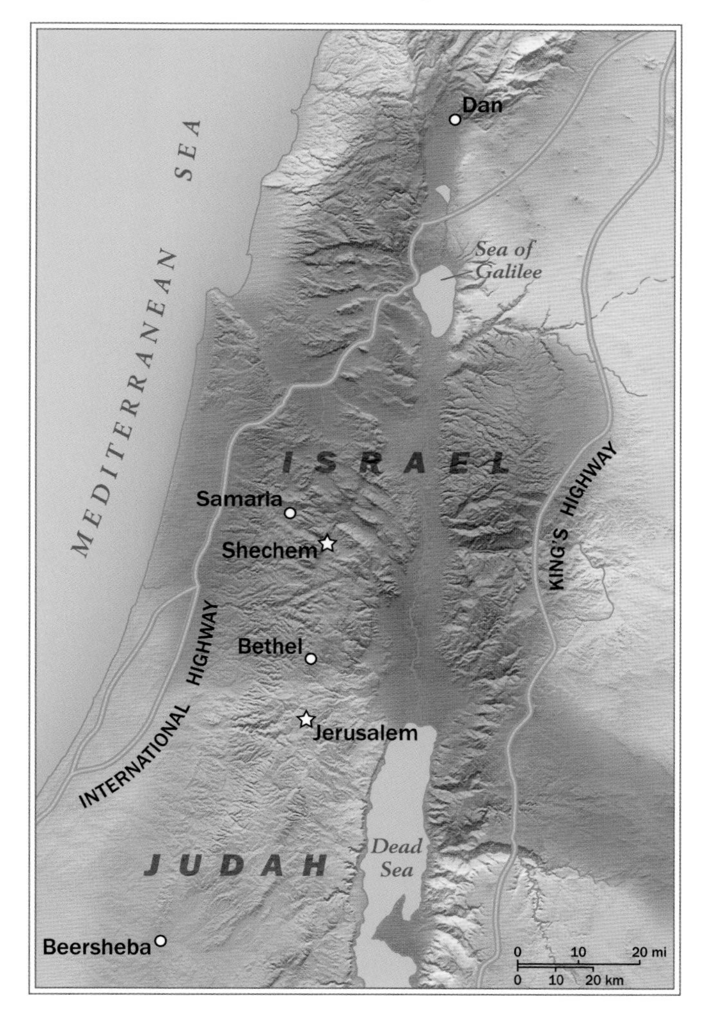

The promised land was divided into two kingdoms, Israel and Judah.

The Babylonian Empire

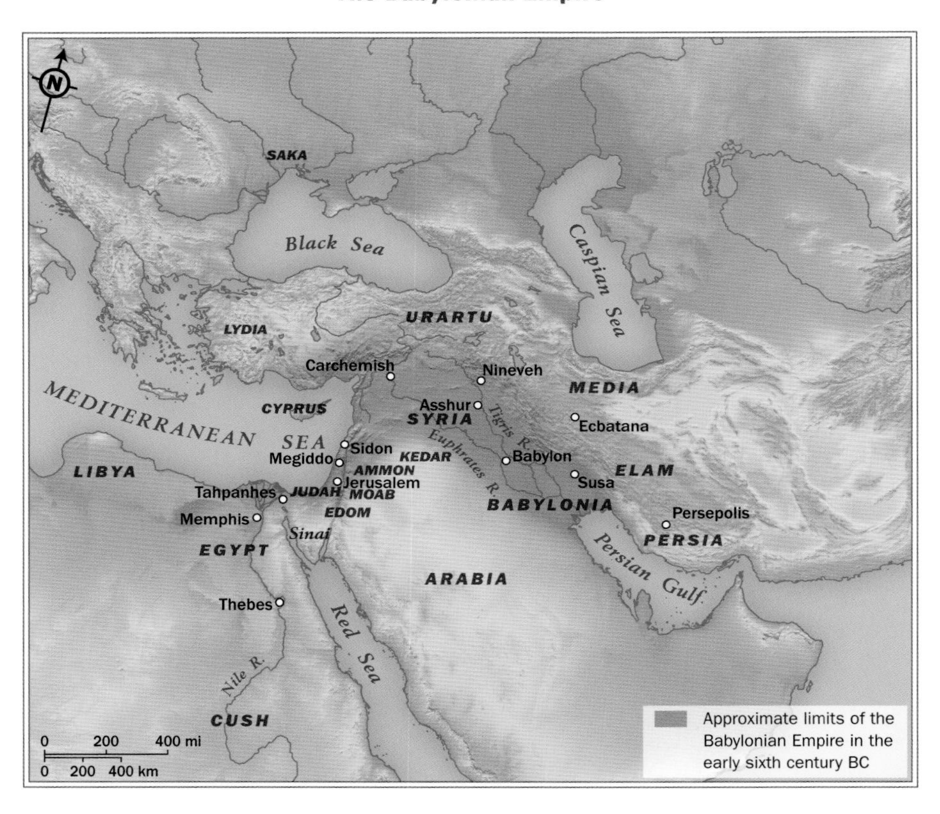

The Old Testament Book by Book

Genesis

Creation, Sin, and Covenant

Central Teaching

God creates the world, banishes Adam and Eve from the garden due to their rebellion and sin, and then begins restoring people to relationship with him through his covenant with Abraham, Isaac, and Jacob.

Memory Verse

In the beginning God created the heavens and the earth. (Gen. 1:1)

Setting

The opening chapter of Genesis takes place at the beginning of time. While we do not know exactly where the Garden of Eden was located, it was probably in Mesopotamia. The story of Abraham (Gen. 12) begins in Mesopotamia. Suggested dates for Abraham vary from around 2000 BC to around 1800 BC. Abraham migrates to Canaan, spends a short time in Egypt, and then returns to Canaan. Later, Jacob (Abraham's grandson) moves to Egypt, and Genesis ends with the family of Jacob living in Egypt.

Message

God brings people into existence, blessing them with life and giving them a chance to know him personally. But we mess it up, sinning against God and rejecting him and his blessings. This action separates us from God and ultimately results in death. God, however, works to restore our relationship with him—a relationship that provides life. This is the story of Genesis and, indeed, the story of the Bible. It is also your story and my story.

In Genesis 1–2, the story begins with God's creation. God creates a wonderful garden and places humankind into the garden where they can have close fellowship with him. How does humankind react to this wonderful blessing? Genesis 3–11 narrates a series of tragic events illustrating how people sin and rebel repeatedly against God, which separates them from God and leads to death. By Genesis 11 the situation of the world is grim. What will happen? How will humankind ever be saved and restored again to close fellowship with God?

Genesis 12 introduces the answer and begins the exciting story of redemption. God makes a covenant with Abraham in Genesis 12, 15, and 17. It is this Abrahamic covenant that provides the framework for God's unfolding plan of salvation for everyone in the world who will believe. The

A view of Africa and the Middle East from space

The Negev, one of the regions in which Abraham lived and traveled

fulfillment of the Abrahamic covenant drives the story throughout the Old Testament and even the New Testament.

The promises of this covenant are passed down from Abraham to Isaac to Jacob throughout the remaining chapters of Genesis. Yet Genesis closes with Jacob and his twelve sons residing in Egypt, with the Abrahamic promises largely unfulfilled.

Outline

- Creation of the world, people, and the garden (1:1–2:25)
- Paradise lost: sin, death, and separation from God (3:1–11:32)
- God's response to human sin: deliverance through the Abrahamic covenant (12:1–50:26)
  - Abraham: the promise and the obedience of faith (12:1–22:24)
  - Isaac: continuing the patriarchal promise (23:1–25:18)
  - Jacob: struggle and the beginning of the twelve tribes of Israel (25:19–36:43)
  - Joseph: faithfulness and God's sovereign deliverance (37:1–50:26)

Interesting Features

- Genesis answers the big questions of life: Why am I here? Who has brought me into being? What is life all about?
- Genesis tells the story of creation.
- God creates man and woman and institutes marriage.
- God makes a covenant with Abraham that impacts the rest of the Bible.

Connections

Genesis is the introduction not only to the Old Testament but also to the entire Bible. Thus the story of Genesis is representative for both Israel and all people. God creates a good place for people to live where they can take part in a close relationship with him. These people, however, repeatedly rebel and sin against God, which results in separation and death. This is the story of humanity. God in his great mercy provides a way of salvation, a story that starts in Genesis 12 with Abraham, climaxes in the New Testament with Jesus, and reaches its final consummation in Revelation 21–22 with the re-creation of the new heaven and earth.

Exodus

Deliverance and the Presence of God

Central Teaching

God delivers Israel from slavery in Egypt and enters into a covenant relationship with them, taking up residence among them in the tabernacle.

Memory Verse

> *God said to Moses, "I AM WHO I AM. This is what you are to say to the Israelites: 'I AM has sent me to you.'" (Exod. 3:14)*

Setting

The book of Exodus begins in Egypt and ends in the Sinai desert. The names of the Egyptian pharaohs involved are not given, so there is no consensus on the exact date of the exodus (either 1446 BC or 1270–1260 BC). The book of Exodus connects to the end of Genesis, continuing the story of Abraham's descendants. Hundreds of years have passed, and the new pharaoh on the throne has no memory of how Joseph saved Egypt (Gen. 41). In fulfillment of the Abrahamic promises the Israelites have proliferated to the extent that they now frighten the Egyptians. Yet the Israelites still do not have their own land, a critical aspect of God's promise to Abraham. The fulfillment of the "land promise" to Abraham drives the biblical story from Exodus to Joshua, where it is finally fulfilled.

Moses's mother hides him in the reeds along the banks of the Nile River. Shown here is a tomb wall painting of an Egyptian hunting birds in the reeds along the Nile (1400 BC).

Message

The message of Exodus can be seen through three interrelated central themes:

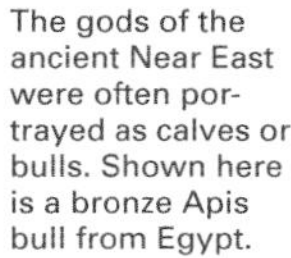

The gods of the ancient Near East were often portrayed as calves or bulls. Shown here is a bronze Apis bull from Egypt.

1. God delivers his people and brings them up out of Egypt. The fundamental message of Exodus is that God saves and delivers his people. Throughout the rest of the Old Testament the exodus event becomes the primary image of salvation.
2. As God delivers Israel he acts in such a way that everyone "knows" and recognizes his power. Those who trust in God will know his salvation. Those who defy God will know his judgment. One way or the other, everyone will know God. There is no middle ground and no way to ignore him.

The Great Sphinx of Giza in Egypt

3. A critical aspect of the covenant relationship that God establishes with the sons of Israel after he rescues them from Egypt is that he will dwell in their midst. Thus the presence of God is a major theme throughout the book. The entire second half of the book (Exod. 25–40) deals with the construction of the tabernacle, where the presence of God will dwell.

Outline

- Deliverance from Egypt (1:1–15:21)
- Inaugurating the Sinai covenant (15:22–24:18)
- I will dwell in your midst: the tabernacle and God's presence (25:1–40:38)

Interesting Features

- God himself appears numerous times in Exodus as one of the main characters.
- Exodus contains a high concentration of miraculous actions and appearances by God.
- God gives the Ten Commandments in Exodus.
- The Passover is first described in Exodus.
- Ironically, Exodus also contains one of the most tragic and rebellious actions by Israel against God (the golden calf episode in Exod. 32).

Connections

The central themes of Exodus echo throughout the entire Bible and are tightly interwoven into our most basic Christian theology. In the Old Testament the exodus event becomes the paradigm (or model) of what salvation is about. Thus, the exodus event is to the Old Testament as the cross is to the New Testament. The story of God's deliverance in Exodus shapes the theological thinking of the entire Old Testament in regard to the character of God and the nature of his gracious salvation. Throughout the rest of the Old Testament, God's favorite way of identifying himself to his people is through the repeated phrase, "I am the Lord your God, who brought you out of Egypt" (Exod. 20:2). Likewise, Exodus stresses the importance of the presence of God, a central biblical theme that runs throughout the Bible, from Genesis to Revelation.

Leviticus

Be Holy for I Am Holy

Replica of a "horned" altar at Beersheba

Central Teaching

The book of Leviticus teaches the Israelites how to approach and worship the holy, awesome God, who rescued them from Egypt and now lives in their midst.

Memory Verse

> ***Do not seek revenge or bear a grudge against anyone among your people, but love your neighbor as yourself. I am the Lord. (Lev. 19:18)***

Setting

In Exodus, God spectacularly delivers the Israelites from Egypt. At Mount Sinai he then enters into a covenant agreement with them. A critical component of that covenant is the promise that God's presence will dwell among them. Thus the entire final unit of Exodus (25–40) describes how to construct the tabernacle, the place where God will live among them. Leviticus is a logical sequel to these latter chapters of Exodus, for Leviticus describes the procedures that will be used in the tabernacle to worship God. Keep in mind that the Israelites were on their way to Canaan, where they were to settle and to use the practices of Leviticus to worship and fellowship with God. Yet the influence of pagan worship in Canaan was very strong. Much of Leviticus is concerned with countering these pagan practices and reorienting Israel's entire worldview toward the God of Abraham, who had just delivered them from Egypt.

An incense altar from the city of Arad

Message

If the holy, awesome God is coming to dwell among them in the tabernacle (Exod. 25–40), how will that change their lives? How can sinful people survive with the holy, awesome God living in their midst? How should they approach him? What is the appropriate way to praise God and thank him for his blessings? How can sin be covered so that the relationship is not severed? The book of Leviticus answers these questions. Leviticus stresses that *everything* in the people's lives will change because now—with the holy presence of God residing in their midst—all of their thinking and acting will revolve around what is holy and what is clean. Within this context, four primary themes run throughout the book: (1) the presence of God, (2) holiness, (3) the role of sacrifice, and (4) how to worship and live within the covenant.

Outline

- Sacrifices for individual worship (1:1–7:38)
- The institution and limitations of the priesthood (8:1–10:20)
- The issue of uncleanness and its treatment (11:1–15:33)
- The Day of Atonement (sacrifice for the nation) (16:1–34)
- Laws for holy living (17:1–25:55)
- Covenant blessings and curses (26:1–46)
- Dedication offerings (27:1–34)

Interesting Features

- Leviticus illustrates the practice of sacrifice, which is essential for understanding the New Testament theology of the cross.
- Leviticus describes the Day of Atonement.
- Leviticus teaches us how serious God is about keeping holy things separate from profane things.
- Four times Leviticus repeats the phrase, "Be holy, because I am holy" (11:44, 45; 19:2; 20:26).
- Leviticus contains the second great command, "Love your neighbor as yourself" (19:18).

Connections

In Leviticus we learn the concepts of substitutionary sacrifice and atonement, concepts that find ultimate application in the crucifixion of Christ. Likewise, Leviticus stresses the matter of clean/unclean and holy/profane issues, which are essential to mature Christian living. Jesus points out the distinction between understanding the issue of clean/unclean as mere ritual and understanding the true issue as relating to what is in one's heart (Matt. 15:1–20; Mark 7:1–23). In a similar way, although we are not saved by our works we are, nonetheless, called to lead holy lives (1 Pet. 1:15–16). The rituals of Leviticus forced the Israelites to view all of life in terms of clean/unclean and holy/profane. We can learn from this. We have the holy, awesome God dwelling within us (1 Cor. 3:16–17; Eph. 2:22) rather than in the tabernacle. Thus we should be even more conscious than the ancient Israelites in Leviticus were of holiness and the need for us to be clean and holy.

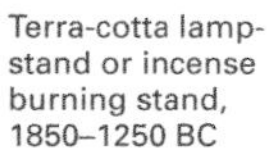

Terra-cotta lampstand or incense burning stand, 1850–1250 BC

Numbers

Taking the Long Way to the Promised Land

Central Teaching

As a disobedient generation of Israelites rejects God's gracious promised land and perishes in the desert, God raises up a new and more obedient generation to inherit and occupy the promised land.

Memory Verses

The Lord bless you
and keep you;
the Lord make his face shine on you
and be gracious to you;
the Lord turn his face toward you
and give you peace. (Num. 6:24–26)

Setting

In Exodus, God delivers the Israelites from slavery in Egypt and brings them to Mount Sinai, where he enters into covenant relationship with them and gives them the law as well as instructions on how to build the tabernacle. Leviticus then explains how Israel should live in light of having God living right there among them. Numbers picks up the story from Exodus. When Numbers opens, Israel is still at Mount Sinai, in the second year of the exodus journey. The setting for the events in Numbers is along the journey from Mount Sinai to the promised land, although the Israelites take the long, "detour" route.

Moses's new wife is a Cushite (Num. 12:1). An Egyptian wall painting from the time of Thutmose IV (1400–1390 BC) depicts Cushites bringing tribute to the pharaoh.

Message

Incredibly, when God brings the newly rescued Israelites to the promised land, they tell Moses they don't want it if they have to exert any effort

An aerial view of the Sinai desert, where Israel wandered for forty years

and faith to occupy it. In Exodus 16:3, the Israelites essentially say to God, "We wish we had died in the desert!" "Fine," God answers. "Go back into the desert and die" (our paraphrase). God leads them back into the desert and allows that rebellious generation to die off. Then he takes the upcoming, more obedient generation and leads them back to the promised land. The contrast between the old disobedient generation and the new obedient generation is immense, and the transition from disobedience to obedience is a critical feature of the book. The two big census lists (Num. 1 and Num. 26) identify and introduce the two differing generations. Numbers 1–25 describes the old disobedient generation, which is characterized by grumbling, doubt, rebellion, and death. Numbers 26–36 deals with the new generation, and the themes shift to faith, hope, and life.

In addition, evidence that God is still watching over his people and still remaining faithful to the Abrahamic covenant runs throughout the book. For example, when Balaam attempts to curse Israel, God intervenes and prohibits it (Num. 22–25). Furthermore, throughout all of Numbers, God engages with the Israelites frequently, supplementing the laws of Exodus and Leviticus and exhorting his people to trust him to deliver them from the enemies that oppose them on their journey.

Outline

- The disobedient generation (1:1–25:18)
  - A hopeful start: God gets Israel organized (1:1–10:10)
  - Israel does the unthinkable—they reject the promised land (10:11–14:45)
  - Israel wanders in the wilderness (15:1–22:1)
  - Encountering Balaam and Moab: God still protects his people (22:2–25:18)
- The obedient generation (26:1–36:13)
  - Generational transitions—the census, daughters, and leaders (26:1–27:23)
  - Reminders of worship, holiness, and faithfulness (28:1–30:16)
  - Conclusion to the Balaam challenge (31:1–54)
  - Preparing to enter the land (32:1–36:13)

Interesting Features

- Moses marries a woman from Cush, an African nation south of Egypt.
- The Israelites reject the promised land and therefore wander in the wilderness for forty years.
- Balaam's donkey talks to him.
- Moses completely destroys the Midianites (his former in-laws?).

Connections

Numbers provides us with a sobering picture of how rebellion against God can set a negative course for a person's entire life. The consequences can be severe. Without repentance, a person can spend the rest of his or her life in the wilderness, going nowhere. Fortunately, the Bible tells us that if we repent and turn to God, then he will restore us and bring us back into fellowship. But as Paul warns in 1 Corinthians 10:1–13, Christ calls us to obedience, not rebellion and disobedience.

This silver amulet from the seventh century BC is inscribed with the priestly benediction of Numbers 6:24–26. It is the oldest known fragment of a biblical text.

Deuteronomy

The Contract between God and Israel

Central Teaching

The book of Deuteronomy is a contract between God and Israel. It defines the terms by which Israel can live in the promised land with God in their midst and be blessed by him.

Memory Verses

> *Hear, O Israel: The LORD our God, the LORD is one. Love the LORD your God with all your heart and with all your soul and with all your strength.* (Deut. 6:4–5)

Setting

The book of Numbers relates the unthinkable story of how the Israelites reject the promised land and how that generation is sent back into the wilderness to wander for forty years until they die.

In Deuteronomy the new generation of Israelites is at the entryway to the promised land. They are camped on the plains of Moab and are just about to cross over the Jordan and conquer the promised land.

A Canaanite god, probably El. Idolatry was the most serious covenant violation.

Message

Deuteronomy is made up of a series of speeches given by Moses just as Israel is about to enter the promised land, the land that was promised to their forefather Abraham. In a nutshell, the book of Deuteronomy defines the terms by which the Israelites can live in the promised land with God in their midst and be blessed by him. This is a gracious offer by God, based on his deep love for his people. Yet God is very specific about how his people will relate to him and receive these overwhelming blessings. God clearly states that he (as Creator, Provider, and King) is the one who dictates the terms of the relationship. God is also extremely clear and unambiguous about how serious he is that they worship him alone. Likewise, he is very clear about how important it is to him how his people relate to each other in their community. If God's people keep these terms (i.e., the laws in Deuteronomy), then tremendous blessings will come upon them. On the other hand, God warns that if they disregard and disobey Deuteronomy, thus abandoning the covenant relationship they have with God, terrible consequences will follow, including the loss of the promised land (Deut. 28).

Outline

- The first speech of Moses: a review of the recent relationship between God and Israel (1:1–4:43)
- The second speech of Moses: the terms of the covenant (how Israel is to live in the land) (4:44–28:68)
- The final speech of Moses: the renewal of the covenant (29:1–30:20)

- The postscript: keeping the covenant during the leadership transition from Moses to Joshua (31:1–34:12)

Portions of thirty manuscripts of Deuteronomy were found among the Dead Sea Scrolls.

Interesting Features

- Deuteronomy is one of the most frequently quoted Old Testament books in the New Testament.
- Deuteronomy contains the Ten Commandments.
- Deuteronomy stresses the importance of worshiping God alone.
- Deuteronomy demands that the people of God love and care for everyone in the community, especially those who can't care for themselves.

Connections

Deuteronomy turns our gaze forward to the prophets and to the New Testament, presenting us with the sobering reality that the Israelites (and we too) are simply unable to keep God's law; thus, they find themselves under God's judgment. The Israelites' only hope lies in God's grace and God's faithfulness to his promise to Abraham, as well as his promise of a new and better system in the future. In the New Testament, the apostle Paul explains this very clearly, underscoring that Deuteronomy demonstrates the need for Jesus and his death and resurrection.

Mount Nebo. Moses viewed the promised land from this mountain (Deut. 34:1).

Joshua

Conquering the Promised Land

Central Teaching

Empowered by God, Joshua leads the Israelites to conquer and possess the land God promised to Abraham.

Memory Verse

> ***But as for me and my household, we will serve the Lord. (Josh. 24:15)***

Setting

The book of Joshua is a continuation of the Pentateuch story. In Genesis God makes a covenant with Abraham, promising him land, numerous descendants, and blessings. This promise drives the story from Genesis to Joshua. At the beginning of Exodus, the population of the Israelites has grown, but they are in slavery (no blessing there) and are not in possession of the land. The story running from Exodus to Joshua is about God delivering the Israelites, blessing them with his powerful presence and the Mosaic covenant, and then actually giving them the land promised to Abraham. Therefore, the book of Joshua is a dramatic conclusion to a long, painful journey. At last, the Israelites are going to enter the promised land, drive out the Canaanites, take possession of this wonderful place, and live peacefully at rest.

Immediately west of Jericho were the rugged hills that would later be known as the Judean wilderness.

Message

The action story line of the book of Joshua is about conquering, distributing, and taking possession of the promised land. The theological story line is similar to that of Exodus, Numbers, and Deuteronomy: obedience and trust in God result in deliverance, victory, and blessing, while disobedience results in tragic defeat, judgment, and the onset of curses. At the heart of the book of Joshua is the proclamation that God is faithful to his promises. He gives Israel the land of Canaan, just as he promised their forefather Abraham.

Important subthemes run throughout the book as well. Closely related to the themes of "land" and "blessing" is the promise of "rest." After wandering for years and constantly waging war, the Israelites will be able to settle down on their own farms and raise their families in peace. Another important subtheme emerges from the long episode dealing with Rahab (Josh. 2) and Achan (Josh. 7): inclusion into the people of God is based upon trust and faith in God, not on Hebrew ethnicity.

An aerial view of the archaeological ruins at Jericho

A final subtheme in the book is the quiet and subtle reminder that the Israelites are not completely successful in driving out all of the Canaanites, something that will come back to haunt them in the book of Judges.

Outline

- How to successfully conquer the promised land (1:1–18)
- A test case: Jericho (2:1–7:26)
- Back on track: the capture of Ai and recommitment to the covenant (8:1–35)
- Conquering the rest of Canaan (9:1–12:24)
- Distributing the promised land (13:1–21:45)
- Resolving conflict among the tribes (22:1–34)
- Renewal of covenant commitment (23:1–24:33)

Interesting Features

- In a book about annihilating all of the Canaanites, the first major story is about the deliverance and salvation of the Canaanite prostitute Rahab.
- The book of Joshua contains the colorful story of Jericho's walls falling down.
- God parts the Jordan River, allowing Israel to cross over on dry ground, just as he parts the Red Sea in the book of Exodus.
- In a book filled with war, the thematic goal is "rest."

Connections

In contrast to the constant grumbling and disobedience of the Israelites that characterizes the story in Exodus and Numbers, the Israelites in Joshua generally obey God (and his servant Joshua). Such obedience results in tremendous blessings, a basic teaching repeated by God and Moses throughout Exodus, Numbers, and Deuteronomy. For us, the New Testament is clear that we are saved by faith and not by our deeds of obedience, yet Jesus still stresses the importance of obedience to his teaching and the blessings that result from that obedience (see especially John 14–15).

Judges

Becoming like the Canaanites

Gold earrings. Gideon's soldiers each give him a gold earring that they took from the slain Ishmaelites.

Central Teaching

The Israelites in the promised land disobey God and turn to idolatry, progressively becoming more and more like the pagan Canaanites they were supposed to drive from the land.

Memory Verse

The LORD said to Gideon, "You have too many men. I cannot deliver Midian into their hands." (Judg. 7:2)

Setting

Throughout Exodus, Numbers, and Deuteronomy, God warns the Israelites that if they abandon him and turn to idols, then he will punish them and even expel them from the land. In the book of Joshua, Israel moves into the promised land, defeating all of the major powers in the area. The leaders of Joshua's generation, those who first entered the land, remain faithful to God all of their lives. Judges picks up the story where the book of Joshua leaves off, just as this first generation to inhabit the promised land leaves the scene. In the generations that follow, the behavior and obedience of the Israelites will change drastically.

Message

The purpose of Judges is to show the failure of Israel to keep the Mosaic covenant (Exodus, Leviticus, Numbers, and Deuteronomy) after God gives them the promised land. Judges paints a dreadful picture of a rapid, downward decline, both theologically and morally. Repeating a terrible cycle, the people sin and turn away from God, which results in a foreign nation overrunning and oppressing them. God, in his mercy and grace, sends a judge to deliver them. The people, however, soon turn away from God again, only to be conquered and oppressed once more. God sends another judge to deliver them, and the pattern repeats. However, as the story moves along things seem to get worse. Most of the judges are tainted in some way and do not measure up in their behavior. Furthermore, not only have the Israelites failed to drive out all of the Canaanites, but they are quickly becoming just like the Canaanites, serving Canaanite gods and embracing Canaanite morality. By the end of the book, the situation is disastrous: a Levite priest becomes a leader in idol worship; the tribe of Dan slides into idolatry and abandons their inheritance; an Israelite city behaves just like Sodom and Gomorrah (the picture of

A decorated Philistine jug, probably used for serving beer

The remains of an ancient gate at Shechem. The city of Shechem and its citizens play a major role in Judges 9.

Canaanite immorality); and the Israelites unite to destroy one of their own tribes (Benjamin).

Outline

- The cycle of disobedience (1:1–3:6)
- The twelve delivering judges and the downward spiral of Israel (3:7–16:31)
- Israel hits rock bottom (17:1–21:25)

Interesting Features

- God gives victory over the Canaanites through two women (Deborah and Jael).
- Gideon defeats a huge Midianite army with only three hundred men.
- All of the judges except Othniel and Deborah are tainted in some way.
- The book of Judges contains the colorful and tragic story of Samson and Delilah.
- The end of the book (Judg. 19–21) is horrific and disgusting.

Connections

Judges illustrates for us the tragic consequences of sin. Once people abandon worshiping God, they usually embrace the corrupt morals of their surrounding culture quickly, spiraling downward both morally and theologically. The most amazing thing about the book of Judges is that the Bible does not end there. That is, after reading Exodus and Deuteronomy it is surprising that the terrible sin of Israel in Judges does not bring about the end of the story—God should simply destroy them. We get a good picture of the depth of God's grace and mercy as we read on and realize that in spite of Israel's terrible sin, God will still send them real deliverers (Samuel, David, and ultimately Christ).

Ruth

God at Work behind the Scenes

Central Teaching

God uses the faithfulness of a humble foreign woman to restore a family to the promised land and to introduce the deliverer who will bring Israel back to God.

Memory Verse

> *All the people of my town know that you are a woman of noble character. (Ruth 3:11)*

Setting

The opening lines of Ruth locate the story during the time of the judges, thus connecting Ruth's story to the disastrous times recorded in the book of Judges. This setting also underscores that Ruth lived in a very unsettled time. It would have been extremely risky and quite dangerous for two women to travel alone across Israel.

By the end of Judges, the covenant as defined in Deuteronomy seems to be completely forgotten, and Israel is worshiping idols instead of God. Thus, several serious questions emerge from the dire situation: "Is there any hope for Israel? Who will deliver them from the mess they made?" The answer is King David, and Ruth serves as his introduction. In 1–2 Samuel, David rises to power and straightens out the mess created in Judges.

Message

The book of Ruth illustrates how God is quietly at work behind the scenes to provide a solution (a deliverer, David) to the terrible situation Israel has created for itself during the time of the judges. In this way, Ruth bridges the story from Judges (disaster in Israel) to 1–2 Samuel (David the hero).

The book of Ruth is not about kings, generals, prostitutes, or priests. It is a story about three simple farming people (Naomi, Ruth, and Boaz) and how God brings them together. When an Israelite family leaves the promised land, curses ensue and all the men in the family die; but when the widows make their way back to the promised land, blessings return. The book of Ruth presents

A Palestinian man processing wheat.

A view of modern-day Bethlehem

Naomi, Ruth, and Boaz as virtuous people, even though they are real people expressing real sorrow over real problems. At its core, this is a love story, with a theologically significant genealogy added to the end of the story.

Outline

- Leaving the promised land results in tragedy (1:1–22)
- Boy meets girl (2:1–23)
- Proposal and marriage (3:1–4:12)
- From Naomi and Ruth to David: a genealogy (4:13–22)

Interesting Features

- Two of the three central characters in the book of Ruth are women, Naomi and Ruth.
- At the center of this book is a colorful boy-meets-girl love story.
- God works behind the scenes throughout the book of Ruth.
- The story ends happily: Naomi and Ruth go from emptiness, tragedy, and despair to happy fulfillment.
- Ruth is called "a woman of noble character" (3:11), the exact Hebrew phrase that is used in Proverbs 31:10.

Connections

We can learn much from the character of Ruth. Faithfulness is a very important virtue in the Bible, and the Lord stresses it throughout the Old Testament. Ruth was concerned more with the welfare of her mother-in-law than she was with her own welfare or personal future, yet in the end, God blessed Ruth tremendously. From her example, we can learn to be faithful in all of our relationships, trusting in God to see us through difficult times.

At the very end of the book, Ruth serves as the introduction to David (a genealogy that eventually leads to Christ). David will be the short-term solution to the terrible situation in Israel that is described in Judges and alluded to in Ruth 1:1. God works quietly behind the scenes through two humble women (Naomi and Ruth) and one faithful man (Boaz) to start the process of raising up a mighty deliverer, David, and ultimately Christ.

1–2 Samuel

The Rise and Fall of David

Uriah the Hittite, the husband of Bathsheba, is a soldier in David's army. Shown here is a Hittite soldier on a wall relief (tenth century BC).

Central Teaching

David rises to power and restores Israel to a proper worship of God, but his affair with Bathsheba tarnishes his reign, undermining many of his great accomplishments.

Memory Verse

> *You come against me with sword and spear and javelin, but I come against you in the name of the LORD Almighty.* (1 Sam. 17:45)

Setting

At the end of Judges the situation is extremely grim in Israel, both morally and theologically. First Samuel opens during the latter years of the judges. Samuel himself is a bridge from the judges to the monarchy, being the last judge as well as the first major prophet since Moses. Saul, the first king, reigns from 1051 to 1011 BC while David reigns from 1011 to 971 BC.

Message

First and Second Samuel are primarily about David, the hero who delivers Israel from the mess at the end of the book of Judges. Samuel's role is transitional; he institutes the monarchy and anoints the first two kings. Saul, the first king, is weak and disobedient. His role in the story is to provide a contrast to David and to remind everyone what happens if people choose their leaders by looking at external rather than internal character. David is the one who gets Israel back on track—the man after God's own heart. He is courageous and he trusts in God. After David becomes king, he completes the conquest, which had been on hold since the death of Joshua. David brings the ark of the covenant to Jerusalem and reestablishes the worship of the Lord God. God even makes a special covenant with David, a covenant ultimately fulfilled by Christ.

Unfortunately, we discover that David is not a sinless messiah but rather a mere man. His affair with Bathsheba and his murder of Uriah are shocking and scandalous. After these serious sins, God forgives David personally but no

The city of Rabbah (2 Sam. 11:1) was the capital of Ammon. The ruins of this city have been excavated in the center of the modern city of Amman, the capital of Jordan.

longer sustains his kingdom, which, along with his personal life, starts to fall apart quickly. We are left looking to the New Testament and to the coming "son of David" for the real Messiah.

Outline

- From corrupt priest (Eli's family) to corrupt king (Saul): the transition from judges to monarchy (1 Sam. 1:1–15:35)
- Who will be king? The contrast between Saul and David (1 Sam. 16:1–31:13)
- The rise of David and the restoration of Israel (2 Sam. 1:1–10:19)
- Humpty-Dumpty's great fall: David and the Bathsheba affair (2 Sam. 11:1–12:31)
- The consequences of sin: the unraveling of David's kingdom (2 Sam. 13:1–20:26)
- The good and the bad: a summary of David and his kingdom (2 Sam. 21:1–24:25)

Interesting Features

- The young boy Samuel is called by God in the night.
- The young man David slays the huge warrior Goliath with a sling and a stone.
- God makes a covenant with King David, promising to put one of his descendants on the throne forever.
- David is portrayed as a real person, with strengths and weaknesses.

The tel at Beth Shan. After killing Saul and his sons, the Philistines hang their corpses on the wall of Beth Shan (1 Sam. 31:8–13).

Connections

We can learn much from David. He is a man after God's own heart, a man of courage who put a high priority on obeying God.

Of course, we also must come to grips with David's great sin with Bathsheba. Sexual affairs can be very dangerous temptations, and strong, committed people like David are vulnerable. We should take the danger seriously and be quick to run from sexual temptation.

One of the greatest individuals in the Bible, David ultimately falls short of completing his mission as king. He is not the Messiah. The tragedy of David's life reminds us not to put our hope in people but rather in the Lord Jesus Christ, who is the true Messiah and who will never fail us.

1–2 Kings

The Rise and Fall (Mostly Fall) of Israel

The Assyrian king Tiglath-Pileser III

Central Teaching

The kings of Israel and Judah lead their people away from God and into idolatrous apostasy, thus bringing upon themselves the judgment of God, as seen in the Assyrian and Babylonian invasions.

Memory Verse

> *But the LORD was gracious to them and had compassion and showed concern for them because of his covenant with Abraham, Isaac and Jacob. To this day he has been unwilling to destroy them or banish them from his presence.* (2 Kings 13:23)

Setting

First and Second Kings are the concluding episode in the story that runs from Genesis 12 to 2 Kings 25, and 1 Kings picks up the story immediately after the ending of 2 Samuel. Thus in 1 Kings 1–2, David (who is old and feeble) dies, and Solomon his son becomes king.

Solomon reigns from 971 BC to 931 BC. After his death, a civil war ensues and the nation splits in two. The northern kingdom, Israel, is destroyed by the Assyrians in 722 BC (2 Kings 17), and the southern kingdom, Judah, is destroyed by the Babylonians in 587/586 BC (2 Kings 25).

Limestone bust of an Egyptian queen (ca. 1550 BC). One of Solomon's many wives is an Egyptian princess (1 Kings 7:8; 9:24; 11:1).

Message

After delivering the Israelites from Egypt (Exodus), God leads them into the promised land. Just prior to entering the land, God gives them Deuteronomy, which contains the terms by which Israel can live in the land with God and be blessed. The driving question that runs from Deuteronomy to the end of 2 Kings is, Will Israel be obedient to the terms in Deuteronomy and thus experience blessing? The simple and sad answer of 1–2 Kings is no.

The central theme of 1–2 Kings is the idolatry and associated injustices practiced by Israel and Judah as they abandon God and the consequent judgment that falls upon them. One of the important subthemes in 1–2 Kings is the dismantling of the spectacular empire and temple that Solomon built. Another subtheme is the reversal of the exodus and conquest. Recall that as the conquest of the promised land began in the book of Joshua, the Israelites entered the land and captured Jericho. In contrast, at the end of 2 Kings Jerusalem is being captured and the Israelites are being driven out of the land.

The ruins of the city gates at the city of Gezer, probably from the time of Solomon (1 Kings 9:15)

Another important subtheme involves that of a remnant. As the nation slides into apostasy and heads for national judgment, the Elijah and Elisha narratives illustrate that hope and deliverance still exist for individuals who trust in God. A remnant will survive.

Outline

- The contradiction of Solomon: splendor and apostasy (1 Kings 1–11)
- Reversing the conquest and dismantling the empire (1 Kings 12–16)
- God sends prophets to confront the corrupt monarchy (1 Kings 17:1–2 Kings 8:15)
- Apostasy and the last days of Israel (2 Kings 8:16–17:41)
- The struggle with apostasy and the last days of Judah (2 Kings 18:1–25:30)

Interesting Features

- Solomon's spectacular building accomplishments are contrasted with his inexcusable apostasy.
- Elijah confronts and defeats hundreds of false prophets on Mount Carmel.
- The Elijah and Elisha stories contain more miracles by God than any other section of the Old Testament since Moses.
- God deals with the bad kings of Israel and Judah in different and unpredictable ways.

Connections

First and Second Kings teach us a great deal about sin and its consequences. If people repeatedly and continuously disobey God and haughtily refuse God's calls for repentance, then they can expect to experience terrible judgment. On the other hand, everywhere throughout 1–2 Kings we see the grace and patience of God as he pleads and waits for the Israelites to come around. Likewise, God pleads with his wayward people today to repent and return to him.

From Elijah and Elisha we learn that individuals can remain faithful to God even though an entire society is hostile to God and his call for righteous living.

1–2 Chronicles

Focusing on the Davidic Promise and Worship in the Temple

Central Teaching

Focusing on Israel's worship of God in the temple and on God's faithfulness to the Davidic covenant, 1–2 Chronicles retell the history of Israel from Adam to the return of the exiles.

Memory Verse

> ***If my people, who are called by my name, will humble themselves and pray and seek my face and turn from their wicked ways, then I will hear from heaven and will forgive their sin and will heal their land. (2 Chron. 7:14)***

Setting

First and Second Chronicles retell Israel's history from Adam to the decree of the Persian King Cyrus (539 BC). Yet the last individual cited in the Davidic genealogy of 1 Chronicles is a man named Anani (1 Chron. 3:24), who was born around 445 BC. Therefore, 1–2 Chronicles were probably written around the year 400 BC. This places the composition of 1–2 Chronicles well after the destruction of Jerusalem and the exile (586 BC) described at the end of 2 Kings. In fact, by 400 BC several groups of exiles had returned to Jerusalem and the events in Ezra and Nehemiah had already taken place.

Message

First and Second Kings conclude the Deuteronomy-based history and looks backward at the failure of Israel and Judah to obey Deuteronomy, explaining why the terrible judgment (exile) came. First and Second Chronicles retell much of the same story with a forward-looking orientation. In essence, the author seems to be saying, "Let's move on."

Thus, 1–2 Chronicles basically cover the same historical time period of Israel that is covered in 1–2 Samuel and 1–2 Kings, but with a different emphasis and a different theological purpose. The

The Siloam Inscription. In preparing for the Assyrian invasion, King Hezekiah of Judah constructed a tunnel to supply his fortress in Jerusalem with water. Faintly inscribed on this stone (taken from the wall of the tunnel) is a description of the construction of the tunnel.

Chronicler (as the author of 1–2 Chronicles is typically called) still acknowledges that Israel's sin and disobedience led to the exile, but he zeroes in on two major forward-looking themes. First he stresses God's divine covenant with David (2 Sam. 7), which promises that a future descendant of David will sit on the throne and rule over Israel perpetually. Since the Chronicler is looking forward and trying to focus on the positive aspects of the monarchy, he skips over many of the terrible sins and failures of the kings in 1–2 Kings, especially the big sins of David (the Bathsheba affair) and Solomon (foreign wives and idol worship).

The second major theme of 1–2 Chronicles is worship in the temple. Much of the focus of 1–2 Chronicles is on the construction of the temple and on proper worship. Thus, many of the kings in 1–2 Chronicles are evaluated on how they relate to the temple rather than how they relate to Deuteronomy (as in 1–2 Kings).

Outline

- A genealogical history from Adam to the return of the exiles (1 Chron. 1–9)
- The reign (or non-reign) of Saul (1 Chron. 10)
- The reign of David (1 Chron. 11–29)
- The reign of Solomon (2 Chron. 1–9)
- The reigns of the rest of the kings of Judah (2 Chron. 10–36)

Interesting Features

- The terrible sins of David and Solomon are not mentioned.
- A strong emphasis on the written word of God runs throughout 1–2 Chronicles.
- The focus of 1–2 Chronicles is positive and forward looking, in contrast to 1 Samuel–2 Kings, which is negative, looking back.
- First Chronicles 21:1 is one of the few Old Testament passages that mention Satan.

Connections

The stress on the lineage of David in 1–2 Chronicles gives these books a messianic tone, pointing forward to the coming of Jesus Christ as the fulfillment of the Davidic covenant. In addition, 1–2 Chronicles teaches us that even if we find ourselves in difficult circumstances, we should trust God's promises and continue to worship him wholeheartedly. Likewise, if we sin, we should humble ourselves and repent, claiming God's forgiveness and moving on in life as we put our sinful past behind us.

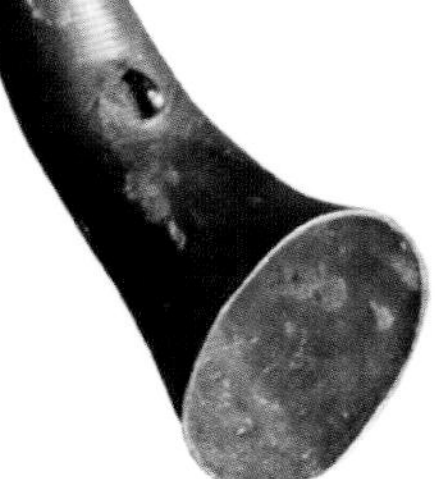

Bronze trumpet (1000–800 BC). When Solomon brings the ark to the temple, 120 priests blow on their trumpets in celebration. Trumpets play an important role in 1–2 Chronicles, where they are mentioned fifteen times.

Ezra

Rebuilding the Temple and the People of God

Central Teaching

Empowered by God and led by Zerubbabel and Ezra, two waves of exiled Jews return to Jerusalem, rebuild the temple, and reform the nation.

Memory Verse

The gracious hand of our God is on everyone who looks to him, but his great anger is against all who forsake him. (Ezra 8:22)

Setting

The book of Ezra picks up the story in 538 BC as Cyrus, king of Persia, issues a decree allowing the exiled Israelites to return to their homeland and rebuild their temple. Ezra 1–6 tells the story of the first wave of exiles to return to Jerusalem and their struggle to rebuild the temple. These events take place in 538–515 BC. In 458 BC Ezra shows up in the story, bringing a second wave of returning exiles (Ezra 7–10). The events in Nehemiah, which are closely related to the story in Ezra, begin in 445 BC.

Message

The two central themes of Ezra are rebuilding the temple and reconstituting the people of God. After the destruction of Jerusalem, the return of the exiled Jews back to Jerusalem and the reconstruction of the temple are nothing short of miraculous. Indeed, the prophets proclaimed there would be a glorious future restoration of Israel to the land. Is this it?

Ezra (and Nehemiah) gives the sobering answer no. This return is not the glorious restoration promised by the prophet. The constant presence of Persian kings throughout the story of Ezra and Nehemiah is a reminder that Israel does not have a Davidic king (as the prophet prophesied). Furthermore, conspicuously missing from Ezra's account of the temple reconstruction is the presence of God. The Lord does not come to fill the new temple with his presence as he did in the tabernacle (Exodus) and the temple (1 Kings), so the glorious restoration must still be in the future.

So what is happening in Ezra? God is setting the stage for the coming of the Messiah. For a Davidic messianic king to come from Israel, the nation must stay intact. Therefore, God preserves the nation, albeit in remnant form. In the meantime, while the people wait for the great coming restoration, those Jews who reside in the promised land are to continue worshiping God. Even though the reestablishment of Israel in the book of Ezra falls short of the restoration promised by the prophet, it is nonetheless a significant start.

The Cyrus Cylinder describes how Cyrus captured Babylon and then allowed the exiles of different nationalities in Babylonia to return to their homes.

One of the many lions made of glazed tile that lined the processional road leading to the Ishtar Gate in ancient Babylon

God has not abandoned his people, and he is moving forward to fulfill his promises.

Outline

- Rebuilding the temple (Ezra 1–6)
- Reconstituting the people of God (Ezra 7–10)

Interesting Features

- Ezra is a priest and a teacher of the law.
- Numerous Persian kings are mentioned in Ezra.
- Although the temple is rebuilt, there is no mention of the presence of God returning to the temple.
- God can be seen working behind the scenes in the book of Ezra, but he does not do any spectacular, public miracles, as in the days of Moses or Elijah and Elisha.

Connections

The book of Ezra teaches us that God is sovereign and in control. Often God works slowly (it seems to us) and behind the scenes, but God has his plans and moves his program along according to his timing and not ours. Our job is to trust God and to continue worshiping him.

Ezra also resonates with us today because God does not work through spectacular miracles in this book (as he did in Exodus). For example, Ezra 1:5 states that "everyone whose heart God had moved" returned to Jerusalem. God did not speak out of a burning bush or part the sea but instead spoke quietly and internally to people who were listening and willing to be obedient. God often works in our lives today in a comparable way.

Nehemiah

Rebuilding the Walls and the People of Jerusalem

Wall frieze of Persian soldiers from the Persian palace at Susa. Nehemiah was probably grateful to have a unit of Persian soldiers with him.

Central Teaching

Led by the Lord, Nehemiah returns to Jerusalem from exile in Persia, quickly rebuilds the walls of the city, and then attempts to rebuild the nation around the faithful worship of God.

Memory Verse

Lord, let your ear be attentive to the prayer of this your servant and to the prayer of your servants who delight in revering your name. (Neh. 1:11)

Setting

In 586 BC the Babylonians capture Jerusalem and destroy it, rounding up most of the surviving inhabitants and forcing them into exile in Babylonia. In 539 BC the Persians, who now control the region, allow the shattered Hebrews to return home. The books of Ezra and Nehemiah tell the story of that return.

The Jews return to Judah in three waves. Zerubbabel leads the largest group back in 538 BC, followed by Ezra with a much smaller group in 458 BC. Nehemiah, appointed by the Persians to be governor over Judah, leads a third small group that returns in 445 BC with the primary goal of rebuilding the walls of Jerusalem.

Stone wall relief of Persian soldiers from the Persian palace at Susa

Message

The book of Nehemiah tells the miraculous story of how Jerusalem is reestablished in the postexilic period. In spite of serious opposition from several powerful neighboring enemies, Nehemiah, the new governor, quickly rebuilds the walls of Jerusalem, thus reestablishing the city as a viable and defensible entity. Rebuilding the people around the true worship of God is probably the ultimate goal of both Ezra and Nehemiah; the temple and the wall are simply means to help accomplish this. Thus the latter half of the book of Nehemiah focuses on Nehemiah's efforts to address internal problems and get the Jews who are back in Judah to follow and obey God faithfully. In reality, rebuilding the nation is probably more difficult than rebuilding the wall. Nehemiah struggles with this endeavor, and as the book ends, it is uncertain whether or not the people are going to remain faithful to God without Nehemiah standing over them, watching.

Outline

- Rebuilding the walls of Jerusalem (1:1–7:3)
- Rebuilding the nation of Israel (7:4–12:26)
- Dedicating the wall (12:27–47)
- Disobedience of the people: Is the work of Nehemiah in vain? (13:1–31)

Interesting Features

- The race to rebuild the wall before Israel's enemies can mobilize and attack is an exciting, suspenseful story.
- Nehemiah prays frequently throughout the story.
- Nehemiah's external challenge (the wall) is easier to deal with than his internal challenge (the faithfulness/unfaithfulness of the people).
- The dedication of the rebuilt wall is celebrated by men and women with singing and great joy.

Connections

Nehemiah seeks to follow God's will faithfully, and he prays frequently throughout the book. Nonetheless, Nehemiah is confronted by numerous difficult obstacles, both external and internal. Even though he is doing God's will, his task is never easy. This is a good lesson for us to learn. Just because God leads us to do a task does not mean that the task will be effortless or simple. Likewise, if a task we undertake for God becomes difficult, this does not necessarily imply that completing the task is not God's will. Sometimes we tend to sit around waiting for God to show us "the open door," assuming that if the door is not easily opened, then it must not be God's will for us to open it. The story of Nehemiah suggests that if the door is closed, then perhaps God wants us to kick it in or find a window. God desires for us to trust in him for empowerment, but he also expects us to plan, lead well, work hard, and persevere in spite of opposition and "closed doors."

The walls of Jerusalem were built, torn down, and rebuilt several times throughout history. Shown here is a current view of the lower portion of the Eastern Wall. The stones to the right date to 164–37 BC, while the expansion to the left dates from 37 BC to AD 70.

Esther

God Uses a Beautiful Young Woman to Save Israel

These bottles held eye makeup, which was applied with a metal rod.

Central Teaching

God works behind the scenes through a beautiful young woman to deliver his people from annihilation.

Memory Verse

> ***And who knows but that you have come to your royal position for such a time as this? (Esther 4:14)***

Setting

The story of Esther takes place in the Persian capital city of Susa, the same city that Nehemiah is residing in at the beginning of the book of Nehemiah. The story of Esther, however, takes place earlier than the story of Nehemiah, during the reign of the Persian King Xerxes (485–465 BC). Xerxes is referred to as Ahasuerus in the Hebrew text, as well as in some English translations. Nehemiah's story takes place during the reign of the following king, Artaxerxes.

Message

The book of Esther contains some unusual features that affect how we determine the message. First, the name of God is never mentioned in the entire book of Esther. Second, none of the characters pray or inquire of God. While Esther does partake of a three-day fast, she never actually mentions God or prays to him (as Ezra and Nehemiah did repeatedly). In fact, none of the characters appear to express specific faith in God, in strong contrast to Ezra and Nehemiah.

What's more, the names of the main characters are disturbing. Mordecai means "man of Marduk." Marduk was the primary god of the Babylonians, making this an alarming name for an Israelite hero. Similarly, the name Esther is derived from Ishtar, the Mesopotamian goddess of love. The meaning of the names, of course, is not conclusive for determining the meaning of the story; but names often do play a role, and these particular names are especially disconcerting. Thus it is doubtful that the author of Esther intended for us to see Mordecai and Esther as models of faith.

Rather, the book of Esther teaches us that even though the Jews who remained in Persia were not strong in their faith, God in his grace

Gold signet ring from Egypt. The king's signet ring is mentioned four times in Esther (3:10; 8:2, 8, 10).

worked powerfully behind the scenes to deliver them from annihilation anyway. Mordecai and Esther are certainly bold and brave, but they do not seem to be faith-driven. As characters, they probably symbolize those Jews who remained in exile and did not try to return to the promised land.

Carved stone relief from the Persian capital city of Persepolis, depicting a king, probably Xerxes

Outline

- The fall of the Persian queen Vashti (1:1–22)
- The Persian beauty contest (2:1–18)
- Haman's plot to destroy Mordecai and all the Jews (2:19–3:15)
- Esther thwarts Haman's plot and turns the tables on him (4:1–7:10)
- The king's decree and the Jews' revenge (8:1–10:3)

Interesting Features

- The story of Esther is an enchanting rags-to-riches story.
- The book of Esther also has an evil villain—a classic "bad guy" named Haman.
- Nowhere in the book of Esther is the name of God mentioned. Likewise, no one in Esther prays or mentions any of the covenants, in strong contrast to Ezra and Nehemiah.
- Esther is never quoted in the New Testament.

Connections

While we can certainly learn much from Esther's bravery, the primary lesson in the book of Esther comes from the actions of God. We see God working quietly behind the scenes to implement his plan. God rescues the Israelites not because of Esther's piety but because saving them is part of his character and his plan, even though the Jews in Persia are not living obediently. God often works in our lives even when we do not deserve it and is faithful to his promises and to his plan in spite of us. This should give us great encouragement in difficult times.

Job

When Life Just Isn't Fair

"Does the eagle soar at your command?" (Job 39:27).

Central Teaching

When inexplicable tragedy strikes, we should trust in the sovereignty and character of God.

Memory Verse

> *Where were you when I laid the earth's foundation?*
> *Tell me, if you understand. (Job 38:4)*

Setting

There is nothing in the book of Job that tells us specifically who wrote the book or when it was written. The actual setting of the story appears to be quite ancient, perhaps during the patriarchal period and well before the settlement of Israel in the land. On the other hand, the book of Job appears to allude to other parts of Scripture (Gen. 1–3 and Ps. 8, for example), and the friends of Job seem to espouse a theology developed from Proverbs and Deuteronomy. This tends to point to a later date, at least for the composition of the book. A plausible setting for the composition of Job is during the reign of either Solomon (971–931 BC) or Hezekiah (716–687 BC), since both of them were very interested in wisdom literature. However, no one knows for sure.

Message

The book of Job is not a list of theological statements that can be taken individually as doctrinal statements. It is a story. While it has a few narrative sections, most notably at the beginning and at the end, most of the story is told through dialogue. The context of each dialogue is important, and the statements of all those who speak must be placed in the overall context of the book. As with most stories, the point doesn't really emerge until the end of the book.

The book of Job deals with the difficult question of how we as wise, godly people are to handle great tragedies that seem unfair or don't seem to have a logical explanation. Four interrelated theological conclusions emerge from the book of Job: (1) God is sovereign and Job is not; (2) God knows all about the world, while Job actually knows

Assyrian wall relief depicting captured camels. A Chaldean raiding party captures all of Job's camels (1:17).

In Job 38–41 God speaks to Job out of a storm.

very little; (3) God is always just, but he does not always explain his justice to Job; and (4) God expects Job to trust in his character and his sovereignty when unexplained tragedy strikes.

Outline

- The testing of Job: an unexplained tragedy (1:1–2:10)
- The search for answers and the slide into accusation (2:11–37:24)
  - Job curses the day he was born (3:1–26)
  - Job and his three friends search for answers (4:1–26:14)
  - Job accuses God of injustice (27:1–31:40)
  - Elihu's hot-air speeches (32:1–37:24)
- God's verbal response to Job (38:1–42:6)
- God's restoration of Job (42:7–17)

Interesting Features

- Job is one of the few Old Testament books in which Satan actually appears.
- God himself appears in the book of Job, both at the beginning and at the end. Toward the end God delivers two long speeches to Job.
- Job challenges the way that God runs the world; God rebukes him only mildly and gently.
- God never tells Job what caused his time of affliction.

Connections

First, when trying to comfort our friends who are suffering from a great tragedy in their lives, we do not want to be like Job's friends, who spend all of their time trying to understand why the tragedy happened instead of simply sitting with Job and hurting with him.

Second, we can apply the book of Job to our lives when inexplicable tragedy strikes us. We should remind ourselves that God is sovereign and we are not. Furthermore, God knows all about the world, while we are unable to see many of the causes and effects or spiritual battles taking place. Also while God is always just, he does not always explain his justice to us; therefore we often cannot understand it.

Finally, and most importantly, God expects us to trust in his character and his sovereignty when unexplained tragedy strikes.

Psalms

Worshiping God

Twelve different psalms mention praising God on the harp. Depicted here is a Mesopotamian harpist.

Central Teaching

God's people should respond to him through prayer and praise, especially in times of crisis.

Memory Verse

> *The LORD is my shepherd; I shall not want. (Ps. 23:1 KJV)*

Setting

The individual psalms were probably written, collected, and organized over a long period of time, and the order of the books is likely due to the chronology of the collection process. There are textual indications within the Psalms of smaller, earlier collections. For example, note the comment at the end of Psalm 72: "This concludes the prayers of David son of Jesse" (72:20). Other collections include the psalms of "the sons of Korah" (Pss. 42–49; 84–88), "the Psalms of Asaph" (Pss. 73–83), and "the Pilgrim Psalms" (Pss. 120–34).

We do not know who actually finalized the Psalms collection into the final form that we have today or exactly when this occurred. Since some of the psalms clearly refer to the time of exile in Babylonia (e.g., 137:1), we can surmise that the finalizing of the collection occurred after the exile, perhaps near or during the time of Ezra and Nehemiah (450–400 BC), but we do not know this for certain.

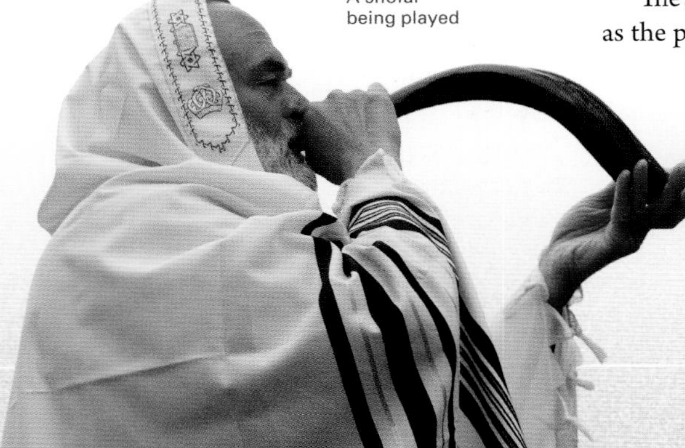

A shofar being played

Message

While the psalms do address doctrine and moral behavior, their primary purpose is to give us divinely inspired models of how to respond to God. The psalms can be grouped into two main categories relating to very different contexts of human life. The first category includes those times when we are doing well, when we simply want to praise God for all of the wonderful blessings he has given us. Or perhaps we simply want to praise God because he is great and praiseworthy. Many psalms guide us in this way.

The second main category can be described as the psalms of lament. A lament is a woeful cry of anguish and hurt. Tragedy can strike without warning or reason, devastating even the strongest of God's people (such as David). The psalmists in general, and David in particular, are brutally honest with God in

Mount Hermon

these situations, pouring out their heartfelt anguish and pain in colorful poetic laments. Usually they use their cries to work through their pain, eventually resolving to trust, worship, and praise God, in spite of their difficulties.

Outline

- Book 1 (1–41)
- Book 2 (42–72)
- Book 3 (73–89)
- Book 4 (90–106)
- Book 5 (107–150)

Each of these five books ends with a statement of praise to the Lord. The entire text of the final psalm (150) is praise to the Lord. Therefore that particular psalm is the praise that concludes the overall collection of psalms.

Interesting Features

- Perhaps more than any other book in the Bible, Psalms connects with us emotionally.
- The psalmist is brutally honest about his emotions—fear, doubt, discouragement, and also joy, comfort, and encouragement.
- The New Testament quotes from Psalms more than any other Old Testament book.
- Psalms contains numerous messianic references.

Connections

The book of Psalms leads us into worshiping and praising God, both corporately and individually. The psalms give us comfort and strength during trying times. They provide powerful, encouraging material to meditate upon during quiet or other personal devotional times.

Yet the psalms of lament also teach us that it is OK to cry out to God in pain and frustration; they provide divinely inspired models regarding how to cry out to God honestly when we are hurting. The psalms teach us that it is OK to hurt, and it is OK to express that pain to God, both privately and publicly.

Proverbs

For Attaining Wisdom and Discipline

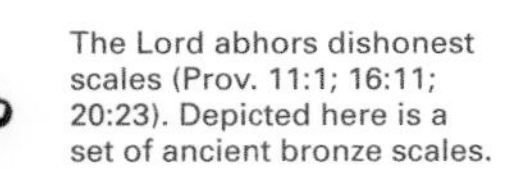

The Lord abhors dishonest scales (Prov. 11:1; 16:11; 20:23). Depicted here is a set of ancient bronze scales.

Central Teaching

Proverbs provides us with guidelines for right day-to-day living and wise character development.

Memory Verse

A friend loves at all times,
and a brother is born for a time of adversity. (Prov. 17:17)

Setting

First Kings 4:29–34 implies that Solomon was familiar with the proverbs and wisdom writings from other intellectuals in the ancient world. While 1 Kings 4:32 states that Solomon "spoke" three thousand proverbs, this verse is not clear about whether he composed these or was just able to recite them. Solomon probably collected proverbs from within Israel as well as from the rest of the ancient world, while also composing some of his own. Under the inspiration of God, a large number of these proverbs were collected, edited, and included in the Bible as Proverbs 1–29 during the reign of Solomon (971–931 BC) and later during the reign of Hezekiah (716–687 BC).

Throughout this process a constant interaction and mixing of folksy, homespun proverbial wisdom from the farms of Israel and intellectual, philosophical reflection from educated scholars (including Solomon) in the courts of Jerusalem probably occurred.

Message

The purpose of the book of Proverbs is expressed clearly in the opening verses: "for gaining wisdom and instruction" (1:2–3) and for teaching both the young and the wise (1:4–5). Proverbs 1:7 ("The fear of the LORD is the beginning of knowledge") connects the successful search for wise living to obedience before God.

A wall relief from the palace at Susa showing a wealthy woman (perhaps a queen or princess) seated with a spindle in hand (cf. Prov. 31:19)

At its core Proverbs is about building character. It provides guidelines for right and wise character development. Proverbs presents the norms of life—that is, things that are generally and normally true, things that one should build his or her character on.

Proverbs presents the norms of life, and the other Wisdom books (Job, Ecclesiastes, Song of Songs) focus on the exceptions. All of the Wisdom books need to be taken together to balance each other. Proverbs without Job can lead to incorrect practical theology, as Job's three friends illustrate. Part of becoming truly and biblically wise is learning how to apply the various proverbial teachings in the book of Proverbs to the differing contexts of life.

Outline

- The proverbs of Solomon (1:1–24:34)
  - — Introduction (1:1–7)
  - — A father's wisdom for the young and gullible (1:8–9:18)
  - — Short proverbs (10:1–22:16)
  - — Sayings of the wise (22:17–24:34)
- The proverbs of Solomon collected by Hezekiah's scribes (25:1–29:27)
- The sayings of Agur and Lemuel (30:1–31:31)

Interesting Features

- Proverbs helps us deal with issues in our daily lives relating to family, friends, and work.
- Proverbs warns against sexual immorality.
- Many proverbs address speech problems (gossip, honesty, anger).
- Proverbs opens with a focus on fathers and sons and closes with a focus on a mother and wives.

Connections

We can apply many of the proverbs to our lives quite easily because they deal with the most basic aspects of life, such as family, neighbors, work, speech, and society. Out of this day-to-day "living in the real world" context several central themes emerge from Proverbs: wisdom vs. folly; improper aspects of speech (anger, gossip, etc.); proper family relationships; laziness vs. hard work; and proper attitudes toward the poor.

Proverbs teaches us not to be boastful or proud. Part of being wise is learning to be humble and concerned about others. We also learn in Proverbs that if we are wise, we will be calm, even-tempered, and slow to anger. We will speak soothing words that calm down crisis situations. We will also be listeners, always ready to learn more wisdom from others and cautious about spouting off our own opinions.

A clay tablet containing Sumerian proverbs (2000–1800 BC)

Ecclesiastes

What Is the Meaning of Life?

"A live dog is better off than a dead lion!" (Eccl. 9:4). Dogs were common in the ancient Near East. Depicted here is a terra-cotta statue of a dog from Cyprus (750–500 BC).

Central Teaching

Meaning in life cannot be found through wisdom, wealth, or pleasure; meaning can only be found through serving God.

Memory Verse

> *Of making many books there is no end, and much study wearies the body. (Eccles. 12:12)*

Setting

The opening lines of Ecclesiastes identify the content of the book as "the words of the Teacher, son of David, king in Jerusalem" (1:1). Any of the kings descended from David could be called a "son of David," so the identity of the actual author is not completely clear. Traditionally, many Christians have understood the author to be Solomon, putting the composition of the book around 900 BC.

Message

Ecclesiastes is one of the Wisdom books (Job, Proverbs, Ecclesiastes, and Song of Songs). Proverbs defines the normal function of wisdom—how to live wisely in the world. According to Proverbs the world is ordered and rational. Life makes sense and operates according to basic cause-and-effect relationships. Job, however, shatters the notion that the logical retribution-based world of Proverbs applies to all situations. Ecclesiastes is very similar to Job, underscoring the exceptions to the norms presented in Proverbs. When the "Teacher" in Ecclesiastes is intellectually and spiritually rattled by things that he sees in life that don't match up to the ordered and logical world of Proverbs, he realizes that a rational and ordered approach to life does not give him a framework with which to grasp the ultimate meaning of life.

"I also owned more herds and flocks than anyone in Jerusalem before me" (Eccles. 2:7). Depicted on this ancient Egyptian wall painting are herds of cattle.

Ecclesiastes is a story about the Teacher's intellectual search for meaning in life using the tools of wisdom (observation, reflection, correlation). Unfortunately, wisdom does not give him any satisfactory answers for ultimate meaning; it merely provides good intellectual tools with which to see the problems and inconsistencies in life. The Teacher wants to understand life and be able to come up with an overarching framework by which he can understand all of life, even the incongruities. His failure to do so is one of the main subpoints of the book (as it was for Job).

The final theological conclusion to Ecclesiastes and the main point of the book, however, is that one should "fear God and keep his commandments, for this is the duty of all mankind" (12:13). Wisdom is a good approach to life and is infinitely better than folly, but one cannot find meaning apart from acknowledging God as the ultimate Creator (12:1). Furthermore, Ecclesiastes suggests that life is not a mystery to be solved and understood but rather a gift to be enjoyed.

Outline

- ▸ The Teacher's quest for the meaning of life (1:1–18)
- ▸ The futility of play and hard work (2:1–26)
- ▸ God establishes order and purpose in the world (3:1–22)
- ▸ Oppression and unjust wealth (4:1–5:20)
- ▸ Wisdom is good, but ultimately it fails (6:1–8:17)
- ▸ The common fate of all (9:1–12)
- ▸ Wisdom is better than folly but still futile (9:13–11:10)
- ▸ The conclusion: remember your Creator and fear God (12:1–14)

Interesting Features

- This book explores various unsuccessful avenues by which people try to find meaning (wealth, hard work, pleasure, understanding, etc.).
- The tone throughout most of Ecclesiastes is cynical and pessimistic.
- The Hebrew word translated as "meaningless" or "vanity" occurs thirty-eight times in Ecclesiastes.

Connections

Ecclesiastes tells us that we will not find meaning in life apart from serving God. Many people today try to find meaning through their work, their lifelong quest to accumulate wealth, or their pursuit of pleasure and/or happiness. As the Teacher in Ecclesiastes tells us, a life lived solely for these goals is meaningless and futile, like chasing after the wind. Regardless of how smart we are or how hard we work, it is only when we serve God that life takes on significant meaning.

A Hittite banquet scene (ninth century BC). Ecclesiastes 2:1–3 probably refers to party-like banquets.

Song of Songs

Wild and Crazy Love Songs

Central Teaching

A truly wise person will realize that the romantic and physical relationship between a man and a woman in marriage is a gift of God to be enjoyed.

Pomegranate fruit. Pomegranates are mentioned several times in Song of Songs (4:13; 6:11; 7:12; 8:2).

Memory Verse

Place me like a seal over your heart,
like a seal on your arm;
for love is as strong as death,
its jealousy unyielding as the grave.
It burns like a blazing fire,
like a mighty flame. (Song 8:6)

Setting

The opening verse in the book serves as a title, "Solomon's Song of Songs." Although some scholars argue that this book was probably written after the time of Solomon, most Christians have traditionally accepted Solomonic authorship. While perhaps it is correct to see Solomon personally involved in developing this "song," it does not mean that this love story is necessarily autobiographical of Solomon. First Kings 4:32 declares that Solomon composed a thousand and five songs. The title "Song of Songs" means "the best song," implying that this song of praise for sexuality in marriage was perhaps the high point of the author's songwriting endeavor. This song is probably an idealized account of newly married lovers, written or collected by Solomon but not necessarily autobiographical; Solomon had one thousand wives!

Message

Proverbs gives good, logical, and wise counsel in advising us to marry someone of stellar character rather than someone who nags or quarrels. Taken alone, however, this advice is not complete. The quiet, prim, and proper demeanor of Proverbs toward one's spouse is fine and appropriate for public life. In Song of Songs, we read that things need to change when the couple is alone at home. A truly "wise" man is madly in love with his wife; both he and she should enjoy a wild and crazy love for each other. The calm, careful, and reserved speech of the wise one

Egyptian necklace (1330 BC). "You have stolen my heart with one glance of your eyes, with one jewel of your necklace" (Song 4:9).

in Proverbs gives way here to passionate love whisperings.

At various times throughout history Christians have interpreted Song of Songs as an allegory about Jesus Christ (the beloved) and his bride, the church. But this understanding is difficult to sustain if one reads carefully. Practically all scholars today concur that this is a book celebrating human sexuality.

The Song of Songs is a series of short songs that a man and a young woman (called the Shulammite in 6:13) sing to each other. Occasionally a group of friends chime in. These statements by the man and the woman (she does most of the talking!) are extremely mushy and corny, particularly to us as outsiders. To those couples who are madly and wildly in love, such intimacies are quite wonderful.

Outline

- The courtship (1:1–3:5)
- The wedding (3:6–5:1)
- The honeymoon (5:2–8:14)

"Look! It is Solomon's carriage" (Song 3:7). This Assyrian wall relief depicts a royal chariot.

Interesting Features

- The Song of Songs contains colorful and explicit poetic language about a husband's and wife's affection for each other.
- The song celebrates sexuality within marriage.
- Song of Songs includes a time of courtship, a wedding, and a honeymoon.

Connections

Song of Songs is a book of wisdom for all married couples, young and old alike. We can apply this book by expressing our love to our spouses with passionate and intimate compliments. The goal of wisdom is to develop character, and as we progress toward this goal we can embrace this model of an expressive and intimate love relationship with our spouses. In public we ought to follow the model of Proverbs and be respectable and reserved. But at home we should follow the pattern provided by these two young lovers in Song of Songs; it's OK to be a little goofy and crazy about each other.

Isaiah

Judgment for Breaking the Covenant but Salvation through God's Coming Servant

Central Teaching

Rebellious sin against God results in judgment, but the coming Messiah will bring forgiveness and salvation.

Memory Verse

> *We all, like sheep, have gone astray,*
> *each of us has turned to his own way;*
> *and the LORD has laid on him*
> *the iniquity of us all. (Isa. 53:6)*

Setting

Isaiah's prophetic ministry in Judah was concentrated in the years 740 BC to 700 BC. During this time Judah is first threatened by an Israel-Syria alliance and then later invaded by the Assyrians. Under constant threat from powerful armies, the crucial question for the kings of Jerusalem is, "Whom will you trust for deliverance from these powerful nations?" This is the context for Isaiah 1–39. Isaiah 40–66, however, is directed toward a later context, written to those Jews who were carried off into exile by the Babylonians in 586 BC.

A colossal human-headed winged bull that guarded the entrance to the palace of the Assyrian king Sargon II, a contemporary of Isaiah

Message

The central message in many of the Old Testament prophets, including Isaiah, can be synthesized to three central points:

1. You (Judah/Israel) have broken the Mosaic covenant; you need to repent!
2. No repentance? Then judgment!
3. Nevertheless, there is hope beyond the judgment for a glorious, future messianic restoration, both for Israel/Judah and for all the nations.

Throughout the book Isaiah stresses justice and righteousness as characteristics of God and the coming Messiah but also as standards for God's people. Isaiah also exhorts the kings of Judah to trust in God when they are threatened by powerful foreign armies. The Lord, Isaiah underscores, is sovereign; he controls history. Thus his people should not fear the dangers confronting them but should trust in God.

Isaiah describes the future restoration as a new exodus, led by the suffering messianic "Servant of the Lord" (42:19), a kingly descendant of David who will bring forgiveness from sin and will restore God's people to relationship with him.

"We all, like sheep, have gone astray" (Isa. 53:6).

Outline

- Judgment, with glimpses of deliverance (1:1–39:8)
- Messianic deliverance, with glimpses of judgment (40:1–55:13)
- Righteous living while waiting on God (56:1–66:24)

Interesting Features

- Isaiah encounters God himself seated on a throne with seraphs flying around him.
- A prophecy is made about a coming child named Immanuel, which means "God with us."
- Isaiah includes the Gentiles in his picture of future restoration.
- The coming Messiah is connected to the Servant of the Lord, a servant who often suffers.
- Isaiah introduces the concept of "new heavens and a new earth" (65:17).

Connections

Isaiah tells us a great deal about God, God's character, and God's heart. Isaiah emphasizes that God is sovereign and in control of history. We live in a sinful, fallen world where terrible things can happen, but God remains on the throne and in control. Eventually God will establish his kingdom, characterized by justice, righteousness, and peace. Thus even in difficult situations we can claim the promise from Isaiah that we do not need to fear.

Isaiah also teaches us that we should not trivialize God or assume that God is indifferent to sin. Disobedience to God, especially if we abandon him or turn away from him, results in serious consequences. God's holiness and righteousness demand judgment on sin. Fortunately for us, Isaiah also prophesies that the wonderful coming Messiah (Jesus) will die in our place for our sin and restore us to God.

Moreover, Isaiah tells us that God cares deeply for those who are suffering, especially those at the bottom of the socioeconomic strata who can't provide for themselves, and that he expects us (his people) to have compassion on and actively care for those in the "underclass" who need help. God wants us to walk closely with him in true ethical and spiritual obedience rather than mere ritual observance.

This clay prism is one of several that are inscribed with accounts of Sennacherib's military campaigns. In general these royal annals are propagandistic and full of political spin. Understandably Sennacherib does not mention the disastrous defeat at Jerusalem, but he does not claim to have captured Jerusalem either. He only mentions his victories over the surrounding cities. Regarding Hezekiah in Jerusalem, the prism states, "Himself [Hezekiah] I made a prisoner in Jerusalem, his royal residence, like a bird in a cage."

Jeremiah

Sin, Judgment, and Deliverance through the New Covenant

Central Teaching

Imminent judgment will come upon faithless Judah for abandoning God and embracing idolatry and injustice, but future deliverance will come through the messianic "new covenant."

Memory Verse

I am the Lord, the God of all mankind. Is anything too hard for me? (Jer. 32:27)

Setting

During the previous several hundred years (950 BC to 627 BC), the nation of Judah became more and more enamored with foreign idols and, as a result, became less and less faithful to God. Not only did they fall into blatant idolatry, but their society also unraveled morally as they disregarded God's call to care for others and to be concerned with justice for all members of their society. Jeremiah lived and prophesied in Jerusalem during the tragic years leading up to the capture and terrible destruction of Jerusalem by the Babylonians. His ministry spanned over forty years, from 627 BC to shortly after 586 BC.

This model of an Egyptian potter was discovered in an ancient Egyptian tomb.

Message

Jeremiah's message is typical of the Old Testament prophets and can be synthesized to three basic themes:

1. You (Judah) have broken the covenant; you need to repent!
2. No repentance? Then judgment!
3. Nevertheless, there is hope beyond the judgment for a glorious, future restoration for both Israel/Judah and the nations.

Jeremiah 1–29 focuses on the many sins that characterize the people of Judah, underscoring how severely they broke the covenant that God made with them in Exodus and Deuteronomy. These sins can be grouped into three major categories: idolatry, social injustice, and religious ritualism. Like a prosecuting attorney, Jeremiah accuses Jerusalem and its leaders of committing idolatry and social injustice. Likewise, Jeremiah declares, religious ritual will not cover unethical behavior or make things right with God. To the contrary, Jeremiah warns, a terrible time of judgment is coming.

Jeremiah 30–33, by contrast, focuses on the coming glorious restoration after the judgment. At the center of this messianic message is the description of the coming new covenant. The remaining chapters

Assyrian wall relief depicting oxen yoked together and hitched to carts. Yokes play a major role in the story of Jeremiah 27–28.

chronicle how the kings and people of Jerusalem refuse to listen and repent, thus sealing their fate. The Babylonians invade, and the book of Jeremiah describes the terrible fall of Jerusalem.

Outline

- Sin, broken relationship, and judgment (1:1–29:32)
- Restoration and the new covenant (30:1–33:26)
- The terrible and tragic final days of Jerusalem (34:1–45:5)
- Judgment on the nations (46:1–51:64)
- The fall of Jerusalem described again (52:1–34)

Interesting Features

- Jeremiah shares his personal fears and discouragements with us.
- Jeremiah connects the coming messianic era to a new covenant.
- The unfaithfulness of Israel in their relationship with God is regularly compared to the unfaithfulness of a spouse in their marriage.
- The judgment imagery of 1–29 is reversed to salvation imagery in 30–33, using the exact same images (e.g., 1–29 speaks of incurable sickness, 30–33 speaks of healing).

Connections

Jeremiah hammers away at the sins of idolatry, social injustice, and religious ritualism, sometimes hitting very close to home. What do we idolize and worship instead of God? Wealth? Success? Fame? Do we live for ourselves during the week, ignoring the call to stand for social justice, and then assume that attendance in church on Sunday will make it all OK? Have we let our rituals (how we do church) replace our relationship with God?

Fortunately, Jeremiah also preaches hope and points those who will listen to the coming new covenant—the time of Christ—when the law will be written on hearts instead of on stone; it is a time characterized by forgiveness. Just as Jeremiah slaps us in the face with the seriousness of sin, so he also offers us the solution by pointing us to Jesus, who forgives our sin.

Incense burner from nearby Arabia (the Sabaeans). Israel and Judah anger God by burning incense to Baal (11:17) as well as to other gods (19:13).

Lamentations

Mourning the Destruction of Jerusalem

Central Teaching

The consequences of sin against God are tragic and horrible, but God's faithfulness gives hope.

Memory Verses

> *Because of the LORD's great love we are not consumed,*
> *for his compassions never fail.*
> *They are new every morning;*
> *great is your faithfulness. (Lam. 3:22–23)*

Setting

Since the southern kingdom of Judah persisted in their sins of idolatry and social injustice, refusing to listen to the word of God through the prophets, judgment eventually came.

The book of Lamentations is a collection of five heartrending songs that sorrowfully describe the terrible destruction of Jerusalem carried out by the Babylonians in 586 BC. A lament is a mournful type of song (akin to the blues) used in the ancient world to express grief and sorrow, often at funerals. In a manner of speaking, the book of Lamentations is a collection of songs to be sung at the "funeral" of Jerusalem. Acknowledging and expressing grief in such a manner also implies repentance.

In the early Greek translation of the Old Testament (called the Septuagint) Jeremiah is identified as the author of Lamentations, and thus it follows the book of Jeremiah. As a result of this arrangement (which was followed by English versions of the Bible), Lamentations not only mourns the destruction of Jerusalem (i.e., the consequences of sin), but it also validates and vindicates Jeremiah's message.

Message

Lamentations 1 personifies Jerusalem as a woman and describes how the city weeps over what has happened to her. Amid the grief and weeping, the chapter contains confessions of her sin but also stresses repeatedly that there is no one to comfort Jerusalem in her grief (1:2, 9, 16–17, 21). This situation can be contrasted with Isaiah 40–66, which promises that the coming Messiah will bring comfort. In Lamentations 1 the comfort is yet to come.

Lamentations 2 and most of chapter 3 poetically describe the wrath of God that fell on Jerusalem. Yet Lamentations 3 is not without hope

Ancient clay tablet from Mesopotamia containing a poetic lament for the destruction of the city of Lagash

"Our dancing has turned to mourning" (Lam. 5:15). In the ancient world, mourning was often a public activity. These Egyptian women are mourning the death of the pharaoh (1319–1204 BC).

beyond the judgment, for in 3:21–26 the song claims hope in God because of his great love and compassion, which are renewed every morning.

Lamentations 4 grimly returns to describing the terrible destruction of Jerusalem and the great suffering experienced in the aftermath. While Lamentations 5 continues this theme, the book ends with a humble prayer to God to remember them and to restore them to relationship with him.

Outline

- No comfort for the grieving widow Jerusalem (1:1–2:22)
- The faithfulness of God in the midst of judgment (3:1–66)
- Sin and its tragic consequences for children (4:1–22)
- Confession of sin to God on the throne (5:1–22)

Interesting Features

- The first four chapters are each structured as acrostic songs, a literary technique that uses the order of the alphabet to structure its poetic lines.
- Lamentations refers to Jerusalem repeatedly as "Daughter Zion."
- The terrible consequences of the Babylonian invasion on children are depicted.

Connections

Lamentations is a stark reminder to us of the serious consequences of sin and rebellion against God. Jeremiah preached and preached and preached to Jerusalem, but no one listened. The people ignored God and hardened their hearts against God and his message. As a result, a terrible and devastating judgment eventually came. This sobering reality is still true for us today. Yes, we live in the era of the new covenant and the wonderful forgiveness provided by Jesus Christ. But for those who reject and defy God and God's gospel message, judgment awaits—a judgment just as heartbreaking, sad, and terrible as that described in Lamentations.

Lamentations 3:21–33 also reminds us of God's great love and compassion on his people who trust in him: "His compassions never fail. They are new every morning; great is your faithfulness" (3:22–23).

Ezekiel

Sin and Salvation: Losing and Gaining the Presence of God

Central Teaching

Because of sin, Israel will lose the presence of God, but in the future the sovereign Lord will send his Spirit, restoring his powerful and holy presence to his people.

Memory Verse

I will give you a new heart and put a new spirit in you. (Ezek. 36:26)

Setting

Ezekiel overlaps with the second half of Jeremiah's ministry. The leaders of Judah disregard Jeremiah's warnings and continue to practice idolatry and social injustice. Thus as Jeremiah predicted, the Babylonians invade. In the first invasion (597 BC) Jerusalem quickly surrenders, and the Babylonians carry off most of the aristocracy of Judah into exile (including Ezekiel). Yet the new leaders in Jerusalem are just as rebellious as the old ones were, and they continue to defy God. Against Jeremiah's advice, they rebel against their Babylonian masters, who respond in 587/586 BC by invading and destroying Jerusalem, carrying off most of the remaining population into exile. Ezekiel prophesies in the context of these two invasions.

Assyrian wall relief showing the king's garden, filled with trees and watered by irrigation channels

Message

Much of Ezekiel's message can be synthesized into three main components:

1. You (the kings and people of Judah) have broken the covenant; repent!
2. No repentance? Then terrible judgment is coming.
3. Nevertheless, in the future God will bring a wonderful time of restoration and salvation.

About halfway through Ezekiel's ministry, Jerusalem is destroyed by the Babylonians, so Ezekiel shifts from warning and judgment to a focus on the future restoration. Within this context two important themes emerge. The first is the sovereignty and glory of God. Even as Jerusalem is destroyed, Ezekiel proclaims that God is still sovereign and will ultimately be glorified.

The second primary theme relates to the presence of God. The most spectacular benefit that Israel received from the old covenant was

A Canaanite "high place" in Megiddo. In Ezekiel 6:3 God announces judgment on the "high places" in Israel.

that God's presence actually dwelt among them, first in the tabernacle and then in the temple. In Ezekiel, due to repeated idolatry and other sins, God's presence is finally driven away from Jerusalem, which is a devastating loss. However, as Ezekiel looks to the future, he describes a time when God's presence will once again be central in his relationship with his people. Indeed, the closing words of the book identify the name of the new city as "THE LORD IS THERE" (48:35).

Outline

- Loss of God's presence and judgment on Jerusalem (1–24)
- Judgment on the nations (25–32)
- God's restored presence and the new temple (33–48)

Interesting Features

- Ezekiel describes the wheels of God's chariot and the strange living creatures that hover around God's throne.
- Ezekiel describes the actual departure of God's glory (presence) from the temple.
- God breathes life back into people who are dead (skeletons), demonstrating that there is always hope and life in God.
- Ezekiel declares that in the future God's presence will be enjoyed in a wonderful new way: God will put his actual Spirit into his people.

Connections

Ezekiel reminds us that God is sovereign, with complete control over history. This should encourage us to not slide into despair when we see evil temporarily flourishing in the world around us. God will ultimately triumph and establish his kingdom.

From Ezekiel we also learn about the vital importance of the presence of God. As Christians we recognize how privileged we are to know God's presence through his indwelling Spirit. This should thrill us, strengthen us, and perhaps even frighten us. Responsibilities accompany the wonderful presence of God that we now enjoy, calling us to live according to God's holy desires for us.

Finally, Ezekiel reminds us that there is always hope. If God can breathe life into those dry scattered bones, he can certainly restore us to a meaningful life in close relationship to him.

Daniel

God's Kingdom Will Not Be Destroyed and His Dominion Will Never End

Central Teaching

Daniel's life and message exhort God's people to live faithfully and trust in God in all circumstances; God alone controls history and will bring about his sovereign reign in his own good time.

Memory Verse

> ***Multitudes who sleep in the dust of the earth will awake: some to everlasting life, others to shame and everlasting contempt. (Dan. 12:2)***

Setting

Daniel dates the beginning of his story to the third year of Jehoiakim (605 BC). The final date given in the book is tied to the third year of Cyrus king of Persia (537 BC). Thus Daniel is a contemporary with Ezekiel and overlaps with the older Jeremiah by several years. Like the ministry of Ezekiel, Daniel's prophetic ministry takes place in Babylon. He lives through the devastating and tumultuous times when the Babylonians completely destroy Jerusalem and carry off most of the surviving Israelites into captivity.

Message

The book of Daniel is comprised of two major units. Daniel 1–6 contains stories about Daniel and his friends standing strong for their faith. However, the major theme in this unit focuses on God, demonstrating that God is more powerful than the kings of Babylon and Persia. The second half of the book, Daniel 7–12, broadens the view to encompass God's great plan for the future, especially in regard to humanity's world empires, as opposed to the establishment of God's world empire. The book of Daniel conveys that, even in difficult times, when it appears that forces hostile to God are dominating, God wants his people to live faithfully, trusting in him and in his promise that he alone controls world history and will bring about his glorious kingdom in due time.

Lions like these, made of glazed ceramic tile, lined the roadway that approached the Ishtar Gate in Babylon at the time of Daniel.

Outline

- Demonstration through stories about Daniel and his friends that God is more powerful than the kings of Babylon and Persia (1:1–6:28)
- God's sovereignty over all world kingdoms and his plan for the future (7:1–12:13)

The ruins of Persepolis, one of the capitals of Persia

Interesting Features

- Daniel contains several riveting stories (i.e., fiery furnace, lions' den) about how he and his three friends remain faithful to God.
- King Nebuchadnezzar and Daniel both have startling and symbolic visions portraying four world empires.
- Daniel sees a vision of the "Ancient of Days" (7:9) seated on his throne, holding court.
- Daniel sees a vision of "one like a son of man, coming with the clouds of heaven" (7:13), an image that the New Testament connects to Christ.
- Daniel's visions pertain to the near future (events prior to Christ) as well as to the far future (events yet to come).
- The book of Daniel is written in two different languages: Daniel 1:1–2:4a is in Hebrew; 2:4b–7:28 is in Aramaic (the language of the Babylonians); and 8:1–12:13 returns to Hebrew.

Connections

The courage and faith of Shadrach, Meshach, and Abednego in the fiery furnace and the steadfast faithfulness of Daniel in the lions' den still stand as models for us today. These men refused to waver in their commitment to God, remaining totally obedient to God in spite of the unpleasant and seemingly overpowering circumstances that engulfed them. These stories encourage us to stand firm for our Lord regardless of the pressure exerted upon us by our culture or by unfortunate circumstances. These men did not compromise their faith, even at the risk of losing their lives. They challenge us to do the same.

Likewise, Daniel's overall message has special relevance to us today. Daniel reminds us that God is sovereign and that his kingdom will ultimately triumph over all hostile world powers—a triumph that includes our resurrection from the dead.

Mesopotamian courts often kept lions in cages so that the king could hunt them. The lions of Daniel 6 are probably lions kept for that purpose. Below is an Assyrian wall relief depicting the release of a lion for the hunt.

Hosea

God's Enduring Love for His People

Central Teaching

God uses Hosea's difficult marriage to demonstrate his deep and faithful love for his rebellious and faithless people, who still will not repent and turn back to him.

Memory Verse

> ***For I desire mercy, not sacrifice,***
> ***and acknowledgment of God rather than***
> ***burnt offerings. (Hosea 6:6)***

Setting

Hosea lived and preached in Israel throughout much of the eighth century BC. In Hosea's later years, the Assyrians grew strong, overrunning and destroying the northern kingdom of Israel (722 BC). In 701 BC the Assyrians even unsuccessfully beseige Jerusalem. Clearly, Hosea lived and preached in a very unsettled and dangerous time. During his early ministry he was a contemporary of Amos and Jonah. Later in his life he overlapped with Isaiah and Micah.

Message

The basic message of Hosea is similar to that of the other preexilic prophets, and his message can be summarized in three central points:

1. You (Judah/Israel) have broken the covenant; you need to repent!
2. No repentance? Then judgment!
3. Nevertheless, there is hope beyond the judgment for a glorious, future restoration.

Like the other prophets, Hosea's indictments against Israel fall into three main categories: idolatry, social injustice, and religious ritualism.

However, one of the major themes running throughout the book of Hosea is the faithful, enduring love that God has for his people. Quite frequently the other prophets (especially Jeremiah and Ezekiel) compare Israel to an unfaithful wife—one who is so promiscuous that she becomes a harlot. In the same way that this figurative woman abandons her loyal, loving husband and becomes a harlot, Israel abandons the Lord and turns to worship other gods. While the other prophets regularly use this literary analogy, for poor Hosea this "analogy"

The Assyrians besiege a city in Mesopotamia. During the later years of Hosea, the Assyrians grow strong and eventually overrun and destroy Israel.

The ruins of Samaria, the capital of the northern kingdom, Israel. Hosea announces judgment on Samaria (7:1; 8:5–6; 10:5, 7; 13:16).

is played out in real life. God tells Hosea to marry a harlot, and he obediently complies. Hosea's wife soon abandons him to become a harlot again, eventually ending up in slavery. God tells Hosea to buy her back, love her, and take her back *as his wife*, thus illustrating in the prophet's life the love and forgiveness that God has for his rebellious and disobedient people.

The book of Hosea ends with a last-minute plea for repentance. If Israel repents and turns back to God, Hosea declares, God will still restore them (14:1–8). The sad reality, however, is that Israel does not repent and return to God, thus bringing on the terrible judgment brought by the Assyrians and then the Babylonians.

Outline

- ▸ The marriage analogy (1–3)
- ▸ The broken covenant and the coming judgment (4–14)

Interesting Features

- Hosea marries the harlot, Gomer, and his relationship with her illustrates God's relationship with Israel.
- Hosea and Gomer have three children, all with very significant, symbolic names.
- The deep love of God for his people is stressed.
- Hosea uses not only the husband/wife analogy but also the parent/child analogy.

Connections

Romans 5:8 states, "God demonstrates his own love for us in this: While we were still sinners, Christ died for us." The story of Hosea paints a powerful picture of the depths of God's love. Even if we have been like an unfaithful and wayward spouse toward God, abandoning our relationship with him to pursue our own desires and oblivious to his constant love for us, he still loves us with a deep and abiding love that continually calls us to return to him. If we return to God, he forgives us and restores us to a wonderful loving relationship, putting us under his powerful care.

Joel

Locust Plagues and the Spirit of the Lord

Central Teaching

Using terrible locust plagues, God warns Israel of judgment coming on them because of their sin and covenant violation, but God also describes the future time of restoration when he will pour out his Spirit on his people.

Memory Verse

> *And everyone who calls*
> *on the name of the Lord will be saved.*
> *(Joel 2:32)*

Setting

Unlike many of the other prophetic books, the book of Joel does not provide any historical heading. In Hosea 1:1, for example, the ministry of the prophet Hosea is tied directly to the reign of several known kings. Thus one can accurately pinpoint the historical setting for Hosea. The life and message of Joel, however, are not tied to any king, and the book does not mention any specific historical event. Most scholars believe that the locust plagues that Joel describes (especially the one in Joel 2:1–11) predict a foreign invasion, either the Assyrian invasion of Israel in 722 BC or the Babylonian invasion of Judah in 587 BC. Therefore, many scholars assume that Joel is prophesying just prior to one of these invasions.

Message

The prophets preach to Israel and Judah with the book of Deuteronomy in their hands. That is, the prophets announce that the people of Israel have broken the covenant agreement as legally documented in Deuteronomy; therefore, they will experience the terrible consequences spelled out clearly in that book (especially Deut. 28). Unlike most of the other prophets, however, Joel skips over the specific covenant violations of Israel (idolatry, social injustice, reliance on religious ritualism). In the opening two chapters he goes straight to imminent judgment. Pulling from Deuteronomy 28:38 and 28:42, Joel describes a terrible locust plague that comes on the land as God's judgment for rejecting and abandoning the laws of Deuteronomy. Yet like the other prophets, Joel also moves beyond the judgment to describe the wonderful time of future restoration—a time when God will pour out his Spirit on all of his people.

Outline

- Judgment through locust invasions and calls for repentance (1:1–2:17)
- The giving of God's Spirit to all his people and judgment on the nations (2:18–3:21)

Middle Eastern locust, similar to a grasshopper

Interesting Features

- Joel presents an extensive and graphic picture of a coming locust plague.
- Joel makes several references to "that day" (see 1:15) or to "the day of the LORD" (see chapter 2).
- Joel prophesies that God will pour out his Spirit on all of his people, an event that is fulfilled in the New Testament at Pentecost (Acts 2:16–21).

Connections

Joel reminds us that sin is very serious and that God's wrath and judgment are a reality that only a fool ignores. On the other hand, the good news of the Bible is that "everyone who calls on the name of the LORD will be saved" (Joel 2:32; Rom. 10:13). Turning to God and trusting in Jesus Christ will save us from judgment.

Comparing locusts to soldiers, Joel states, "They charge like warriors; they scale walls like soldiers. They all march in line, not swerving from their course" (2:7).

In addition, one of the central promises of the Old Testament is the promise of God's presence ("I will dwell among them"; Exod. 25:8), a reality experienced through his residence in the tabernacle and then in the temple. However, because of their sin and disobedience, the Israelites lose the empowering presence of God (Ezek. 8–10). In the future, Joel proclaims, all God's people will enjoy the power and comfort of God's presence in a new and better way—through his indwelling Spirit! This promise is fulfilled in the New Testament, and all those who believe in Jesus Christ experience the power and comfort of the presence of God in their lives because the Spirit of God dwells within them.

Amos

The Severe Consequences of Injustice

Central Teaching

Because Israel is worshiping idols and regularly practicing social injustice, judgment is coming.

Memory Verse

> *But let justice roll on like a river,*
> *righteousness like a never-failing stream.*
> *(Amos 5:24)*

Setting

Amos raised sheep and figs and came from a village called Tekoa, about ten miles south of Jerusalem. This fact locates Amos in the southern kingdom of Judah. Ironically, he delivered his scathing criticism and pronouncement of judgment to those in the northern kingdom of Israel. The ministry of Amos is dated to the reign of Uzziah, king of Judah (783–742 BC), and Jeroboam II, king of Israel (786–746 BC). At the time of Amos the northern kingdom of Israel was powerful and prosperous, but that prosperity was limited to the upper classes. The religious situation in Israel was terrible; they had turned away from God and built pagan altars with calf idols at worship centers such as Bethel, Dan, and Gilgal. By the time of Amos, the northern kingdom of Israel was well entrenched in idolatry and the corrupt moral behavior that went along with it.

An ancient pair of sandals. Twice Amos decries the fact that the needy were being bought and sold for a pair of sandals (2:6; 8:6).

Message

In general, Amos delivers the same basic three-part message that the rest of the preexilic prophets proclaim:

1. You have broken the covenant; you need to repent!
2. No repentance? Then judgment!
3. Nevertheless, there is hope beyond the judgment for a glorious, future restoration, both for Israel/Judah and for the nations.

Directing his message primarily toward the northern kingdom Israel, Amos focuses mainly only on points 1 and 2 (sin and judgment). Also, while many of the other prophets sprinkle in passages of hope and restoration throughout their messages of judgment, Amos makes no mention of hope or restoration until the very end of the book, where the prophet finally gives a few verses of hope regarding the coming Davidic Messiah (9:11–15).

The theme that occurs repeatedly throughout Amos is

God's concern for social justice. When Israel ignores the law of God and breaks away from an obedient relationship with him, they soon lose all sense of ethical concern, creating a situation in which corruption and exploitation by the rich and powerful run unabated. Amos is unrelenting in his criticism of these people and the situation they have created.

Israelite altars from Arad (tenth to seventh century BC). Amos declares that God wants social justice, not hypocritical ritual.

Outline

- Social injustice and judgment (1:2–9:10)
- The coming Davidic Messiah and restoration (9:11–15)

Interesting Features

- Amos is a rustic farmer who blasts the wealthy.
- The theme of social justice ("Let justice roll on like a river" [5:24]) is repeatedly stressed.
- Amos uses colorful yet scathing language (e.g., he compares the wealthy women in Israel to cows [4:1]).
- Amos portrays God in his wrath as a hungry, devouring lion.

Connections

Amos is unrelenting in his challenge regarding our concern for those who suffer. Throughout the book, God repeatedly reveals his heart in this matter. God is indignant and impatient with those who enjoy living in luxury while the poor around them suffer in poverty. God expects his people to show the same compassion that he does for the poor and others who suffer. What's more, God gets particularly upset when we separate ourselves from the plight of the poor and focus on enjoying our high standard of living. If we disregard the suffering of others, God views our worship of him as hypocritical, and it does not please him. God does not want our hypocritical worship, which is separated from empathy and compassion for others; rather, God wants us to care for people and to work to alleviate suffering. As we do this we truly come to know God and worship him properly, for our hearts are aligned with his.

Obadiah

The End of Edom

Central Teaching

The nation of Edom, which represents those who oppose God, will be judged and destroyed, while Israel will be restored.

Memory Verse

> *The day of the LORD is near*
> *for all nations. (Obad. 15)*

Setting

The nation of Edom was adjacent to Judah, located to the southeast. Edom often conspired with Judah against the larger empires, but when the Babylonians invaded Judah and Babylonian victory seemed unstoppable, Edom switched sides and joined the Babylonians in plundering Judah. Obadiah prophesies that Edom will be destroyed for betraying and attacking Judah.

Immediately before the book of Obadiah, Amos 9:12 mentions Edom. Obadiah is probably situated directly after Amos because of this connection. While Edom was a real nation that was indeed destroyed, the authors of the Bible occasionally use Edom as a symbol of all those who oppose God and his people (see Joel 3:19; Amos 1:11–12; 9:12). The book of Obadiah is likely using Edom in both senses.

The name Obadiah means "servant of the Lord." It is a very common name in the Old

The rugged terrain of Edom

Testament, used for thirteen different people. The prophet Obadiah prophesies shortly after the fall of Jerusalem in 586 BC, so he was a contemporary of Jeremiah and Zephaniah. Other than that, we know very little about him.

Message

Most of the other prophets proclaim a similar three-part message, which is directed primarily at Israel/Judah:

1. You have broken the covenant. Repent!
2. No repentance? Then judgment.
3. Nevertheless, there is a future hope for your restoration.

Obadiah, by contrast, is quite different. He does not preach directly to Israel or Judah but instead addresses the nation of Edom. Obadiah is short—only one brief chapter—and his message is focused on Edom. Judgment, Obadiah proclaims, is coming to Edom because of their sin.

Because the nation of Edom betrayed Judah and assisted in plundering her, Obadiah prophesies the destruction of Edom. The prophets often declare judgment on the various nations, but usually those same nations are also mentioned in the prophetic picture of future restoration, which includes the gentiles as part of the people of God. The situation for Edom, however, appears to be different. Obadiah (as well as several of the other prophets) proclaims the end of Edom. Edom will be destroyed and will never be restored. Obadiah then proclaims that Israel, by contrast, will be restored in the future and will actually rule over the region once controlled by Edom (vv. 17–21).

Outline

- Judgment of Edom's arrogance and sin (1–14)
- Edom destroyed, Israel restored (15–21)

The Nabateans displaced the Edomites and built the spectacular city of Petra, shown here.

Interesting Features

- Obadiah is the shortest book in the Old Testament (only twenty-one verses).
- Obadiah applies the "day of the Lord" judgment to Edom.
- The colorful description of Edom in Obadiah 3–4 aptly describes the area occupied by the spectacular ruins of Petra, built by the people who destroyed and displaced the Edomites.

Connections

The short book of Obadiah is a reminder that sin has consequences and that God will ultimately judge all those who oppose him and rebel against him. However, God's people will be restored and ultimately vindicated. In this sense Obadiah's message connects to the book of Revelation, which incorporates the same theme into the climactic end of human history, when God establishes his kingdom.

Jonah

Concern for the Salvation of the Gentiles

Central Teaching

A reluctant prophet preaches to the pagan Ninevites, who repent of their sin and are delivered.

Memory Verse

> *When God saw what they did and how they turned from their evil ways, he relented and did not bring on them the destruction he had threatened. (Jon. 3:10)*

Setting

The book of Jonah itself does not tie the prophet's message to a specific historical setting, but the book does identify the prophet as "Jonah, son of Amittai," a prophet who is also mentioned in 2 Kings 14:25. From 2 Kings 14, Jonah can be dated to the reign of Jeroboam II (786–746 BC), thus making him a contemporary of Hosea and Amos.

During the reign of Jeroboam II the nation of Israel was fairly strong and prosperous. In the generation following Jeroboam II, the Assyrians rose to power and subdued almost every nation in the region. During the time of Jonah, however, the Assyrians were still somewhat unstable and relatively weak, certainly no stronger than the Israelites. Nineveh was the capital of Assyria, and even by the time of Jonah the Assyrians had achieved a reputation as brutal and vicious warriors.

An ancient ship anchor

Message

Jonah is a book about obedience that illustrates how foolish it is to refuse to obey God or to try to flee from God and his calling. Jonah is also a book about compassion and concern for one's enemies or for those who are simply different. God had compassion on the Assyrians in Nineveh, and he rebukes Jonah for his lack of concern over their salvation. What's more, the book of Jonah underscores how serious and outrageous it was for the Israelites in Jerusalem to ignore the prophetic call to repent and return to God. The repentant actions of the Assyrians in Nineveh—from the king to the lowest peasant (and even the cows!)—lead to their deliverance, which contrasts with the obstinate, hostile, and unrepentant attitude of the kings and people in Israel and Judah.

Outline

- Jonah, the sailors, and deliverance (1–2)
- Jonah, the Ninevites, and deliverance (3–4)

Interesting Features

- Jonah is very different from the other prophets (he disobeys God, his audience listens to him, he pouts when people are saved, etc.).

Scene from an Assyrian wall relief portraying the horrific consequences for the inhabitants of the Judean city Lachish after being conquered by the Assyrians

- Jonah is swallowed by a large fish, which symbolizes both deliverance and judgment.
- The events of Jonah 1–2 are paralleled by the events of Jonah 3–4.
- Jonah's spoken message (only one verse long) is directed to the Ninevites, but the literary message is probably directed to Israel.

Connections

One of the obvious applications that can be made from the book of Jonah is that if God tells us to do something or to go somewhere we should be obedient. If God calls us into a specific work or ministry, we are foolish if we think we can run away from him and the task he has called us to.

Another central lesson for us today is the realization that God's compassion is boundless; God loves everybody (even the cruel and violent Assyrians). One of the major themes running throughout the Bible is that God saves the most unlikely people (the Canaanite Rahab, the Moabite Ruth, and the entire city of Assyrian Ninevites).

Likewise, the story of Jonah is an indictment against us if we are more concerned with our own well-being than with the plight of those who are lost. To use the plant analogy in Jonah 4, are we more concerned about our lawn dying than our neighbors perishing?

Micah

Justice, Judgment, and Hope for the Future

"They will beat their swords into plowshares" (Mic. 4:3). Pictured here are an ancient sword and an ancient plowshare.

Central Teaching

Because of the idolatry and unjust lifestyles of Israel and Judah, God judges them. Yet beyond the judgment a deliverer is coming to restore God's people.

Memory Verse

> *He has showed you, O mortal, what is good.*
> *And what does the LORD require of you?*
> *To act justly and to love mercy*
> *and to walk humbly with your God.*
> *(Mic. 6:8)*

Setting

Micah overlapped with Isaiah, Amos, and Hosea, prophesying during the reigns of Jotham, Ahaz, and Hezekiah (in the latter years of the 700s, or eighth century, BC). In 722 BC the Assyrians conquered the northern kingdom of Israel and completely destroyed the capital Samaria. Then in 701 BC the Assyrians laid siege to Jerusalem, but the Lord intervened for King Hezekiah and defeated them (2 Kings 17–20; Isa. 36–39). Micah preached in this context.

Message

The name Micah means "who is like the Lord." Micah cries out for justice in the land. He is particularly critical of Israel's leaders and their lack of justice. As a result of the lack of justice and due to the pervasive idolatry in Israel and Judah, Micah declares that the judgment of God is coming (the Assyrian invasion). However, Micah also declares a glorious time in the future when God will send a deliverer and restore his people.

Micah is a typical preexilic prophet, and the essence of his message falls in line with the three standard themes of the prophets:

1. You (Judah/Israel) have broken the covenant; you need to repent!
2. No repentance? Then judgment!
3. Nevertheless, there is hope beyond the judgment for a glorious, future restoration, both for Judah/ Israel and for the nations.

Dominating the historical background for Micah is the expanding Assyrian Empire. Pictured here from a wall relief in Sennacherib's palace is a scene of captured people being deported.

The Church of the Nativity in Bethlehem. Micah prophesies that the coming Deliverer/Shepherd will come from Bethlehem (5:2).

As in many of the other prophetic books, when Micah declares that Israel and Judah have broken the covenant, he focuses on three major sins: idolatry, social injustice, and religious ritualism. Likewise (in keeping with the other prophetic books), the book of Deuteronomy provides the theological background for Micah's message. When Micah declares that Israel and Judah have broken the covenant, he is referring to the covenant as formulated in Deuteronomy.

Outline

- Judgment, yet promise for the future (1–2)
- Justice, leadership, and the Coming One (3–5)
- Life in the present and hope for the future (6–7)

Interesting Features

- Micah presents a very colorful wordplay on various cities (1:10–15).
- Micah prophesies that the future Deliverer/ Shepherd will come from Bethlehem (5:2).
- Micah uses the powerful imagery of hammering swords into plowshares to symbolize the peace that the Messiah will bring (4:3).

Connections

Micah 6:6–8 is especially applicable today. What does God want from us? Is ritual enough (e.g., extensive church attendance)? Obviously not. God wants our lives to be characterized by justice and a deep, zealous desire for love and mercy as we live day by day in close relationship with him, humbly recognizing him as our Creator and Savior. Only in this context do our rituals (how we do church) have meaning and reflect true worship and adoration of God.

Micah's clear identification of Bethlehem as the place where the coming Messiah will be born (5:2) illustrates the powerful predictive aspect of the Old Testament prophets, confirming that Jesus is indeed the fulfillment of the Old Testament. This should encourage us to trust in God, who clearly has control of history and is moving to bring about his plan.

Nahum

The End of Nineveh

Central Teaching

God is going to destroy Nineveh, the capital of the Assyrians, because of their brutal subjugation of other nations.

Memory Verse

The Lord is good,
a refuge in times of trouble.
He cares for those who trust in him. (Nah. 1:7)

Setting

The twelve Minor Prophets are interrelated, and they often serve to balance and complement each other. During the reign of Jeroboam II (786–746 BC), as recorded in the nearby book of Jonah, the city of Nineveh repents and escapes the judgment of God. The book of Nahum reveals that the repentance of Nineveh was apparently short lived. In the latter half of the eighth century and throughout the first half of the seventh century, the Assyrians (whose capital was at Nineveh) continued to grow in power and ferocity, expanding their empire all the way to Egypt. They completely destroyed the northern kingdom of Israel in 722 BC and unsuccessfully besieged Jerusalem in 701 BC. The Major Prophets Isaiah, Jeremiah, and Ezekiel all contain sections that prophesy judgment on the powerful nations of the region. Nahum functions somewhat similarly within the Book of the Twelve (the Minor Prophets), announcing judgment on the dominant world power of the day, Assyria.

The temple-filled city of Thebes in Egypt was destroyed by the Assyrians in 663 BC. Nineveh was destroyed by the Babylonians in 612 BC. Nahum writes in between these two

Nahum asks the Ninevites, "Are you better than Thebes?" (3:8). He is referring to the destruction of the city of Thebes, which the Assyrians had destroyed a few years before. These figures are part of the extensive remains of Thebes.

Here is a pleasant scene from a wall relief of the Assyrian king Ashurbanipal. He and his wife are dining to music in the garden, but note the grisly head of one of his enemies hanging in the tree to the left.

events—after the fall of Thebes but before the fall of Nineveh. At this time in history the brutal Assyrians dominated the ancient Near East.

Message

Nahum proclaims judgment on the Assyrians and the destruction of their capital city, Nineveh. In the opening verses Nahum declares that the Lord will bring about judgment on his enemies, and throughout the book Nahum describes the coming judgment on Nineveh, using colorful and graphic language. For example, in 2:11 he compares the destruction of Nineveh to the ruination of a lions' den; the cubs and the lioness can no longer safely eat where they once did. Nahum ends the book by saying that everyone who hears about the fall of Assyria will clap their hands in joy because they have all felt the cruel hand of the Assyrian army.

Outline

- God's wrath against his enemies like Nineveh (1:1–11)
- Destruction in Nineveh, restoration and peace in Judah (1:12–15)
- The attack and destruction of Nineveh (2:1–3:19)

Interesting Features

- Nahum taunts the king of Assyria with the coming judgment: "All who hear the news about you clap their hands at your fall" (3:19).
- Nahum mentions the destruction of the Egyptian city of Thebes, an important event in Egyptian history.
- Nahum balances out the book of Jonah, where the Ninevites escape judgment by repenting.

Connections

Nahum is a reminder that God ultimately brings about judgment and punishment on those who oppose him and oppress his people. In the book of Jonah, God responds with compassion and forgiveness for the people of Nineveh when they humble themselves, fast, cease from doing evil deeds, and cry out to God for deliverance. However, as time passes and Assyria becomes a brutal, vicious, empire-building nation, God's wrath is aroused. Because the current generation lacks repentance, God judges them, using the Babylonians to destroy Nineveh just as Nahum predicted.

Habakkuk

Talking with God about Judgment

Rhytons, large cup-bowl vessels made for mixing and drinking wine, have been found in numerous archaeological sites. This one was found in Syria (fifth century BC). Habakkuk, as well as several other prophets, uses the image of drinking wine as one of judgment. He declares, "The cup from the LORD's right hand is coming around to you" (2:16).

Central Teaching

Habakkuk questions God but then learns to accept God's sovereign plan of raising up the Babylonians to judge the injustices and idolatry of Judah.

Memory Verse

> ***But the righteous person will live by his faithfulness. (Hab. 2:4)***

Setting

The book of Habakkuk does not have an opening historical superscription tying it to the reign of a certain king, but Habakkuk 1:6 indicates that the setting for Habakkuk is in the southern kingdom of Judah just prior to one of the Babylonian invasions (597 BC or 587/586 BC). This would make Habakkuk a contemporary of Jeremiah and Zephaniah. Josiah, the last good king of Judah, was killed by an Egyptian army in 609 BC, and the kings who succeeded him, along with the nobles and most of the priests and court prophets (i.e., false prophets), quickly led the nation into a moral and theological decline. The book of Jeremiah provides a good picture of the blatant idolatry and social injustice that characterized Jerusalem in the time of Habakkuk. The prophet Habakkuk is one of the few people, along with the other true prophets such as Jeremiah and Zephaniah, who react against this degeneration.

Wall relief depicting Assyrian cavalry

Message

Sometimes we look at the evil and sin around us and wonder why God doesn't do something about it. This is exactly what the prophet Habakkuk did. He saw terrible things in his home country of Judah, and he complained to God, "Why do you make me look at injustice? Why do you tolerate wrong?" (1:3). The book of Habakkuk deals with how God answers Habakkuk and how the prophet comes to grips with that answer.

In essence Habakkuk follows the standard three-part prophetic message:

1. You (Judah) have broken the covenant; you need to repent!
2. No repentance? Then judgment!
3. Nevertheless, there is hope beyond the judgment for a glorious, future restoration.

However, the style of Habakkuk is quite different than the other prophetic books because the book of Habakkuk is structured as a dialogue between Habakkuk and God.

Outline

- Habakkuk asks God: Why don't you do something about the injustice in Judah? (1:1–4).
- God answers Habakkuk: I am doing something—raising up the Babylonians (1:5–11).
- Habakkuk asks a follow-up question: How can that be right? They are worse than we are (1:12–2:1).
- God responds to Habakkuk: This judgment is certainly coming (2:2–20).
- Habakkuk makes a final, concluding statement: I will wait for the judgment and rejoice in God (3:1–19).

Interesting Features

- The book of Habakkuk is a dialogue between the prophet and God.
- Habakkuk struggles with why God allows injustice to persist in Judah.
- In the New Testament Paul uses Habakkuk 2:4 as a foundational verse for explaining justification by faith (Rom. 1:17; Gal. 3:11).
- Habakkuk learns to rejoice in God, even though judgment is coming on Judah, his home country.

Connections

Habakkuk teaches us that often we do not understand how God is working. Sometimes, like Habakkuk, we ask why God does not intervene and do something right now. This book tells us to trust in God's long-range plan and to wait patiently in the meantime, rejoicing in God's control of the outcome.

In addition, as Paul so eloquently explains in Romans and Galatians, faith in God is a critical component of a true relationship with God and should be a central feature in our day-to-day understanding of how God works in the world. Faith, life, and salvation are inextricably bound up together.

The book of Habakkuk is set just prior to the Babylonians' rise to power. This clay tablet gives a description of the Babylonian capture of Nineveh, the Assyrian capital, a critical event in the shift in power from Assyria to Babylonia.

Zephaniah

The Day of the Lord Is Near

Central Teaching

The "day of the LORD" is coming—a time of judgment on God's enemies but also a time of restoration and blessing on those who trust in him.

Memory Verse

The LORD your God is with you,
the Mighty Warrior who saves.
He will take great delight in you;
in his love he will no longer rebuke you,
but will rejoice over you with singing.
(Zeph. 3:17)

Setting

Zephaniah 1:1 places the ministry of Zephaniah during the reign of Josiah, the last good king of Judah (640–609 BC) and one of the few kings of Judah who obeyed God and worshiped him alone. Thus Zephaniah's ministry overlapped with the early years of Jeremiah.

At the beginning of Josiah's reign, the Assyrians still dominated the region, having driven the Cushites out of Egypt and destroyed Thebes, the center of Cushite religious domination of Egypt (see Nah. 3:8–10). But to the east of Assyria, the Babylonians rose to power. By the end of Josiah's reign the Assyrians were in retreat, and the Babylonians were aggressively expanding.

Message

Like the other preexilic prophets, Zephaniah's basic message can be synthesized to the three standard prophetic themes:

1. You (Judah) have broken the covenant; you need to repent!
2. No repentance? Then judgment!
3. Nevertheless, there is hope beyond the judgment for a glorious, future restoration, both for Israel/Judah and for the nations.

Zephaniah accuses Judah of the same basic covenant violations that the other prophets rage against—idolatry, social injustice, and religious ritualism. Zephaniah also refers frequently to the "day of the LORD," a time of judgment on God's enemies—that is, those who oppose God, oppress his people, or rebel against him. It is also a time of judgment on Israel and Judah for their rejection of God and their terrible sins against the covenant.

Clay cylinder with an inscription of Nebuchadnezzar recording how he repaired a temple to Shamash, the sun god

Zephaniah preaches judgment on the cities of Philistia (2:4–7). Pictured are the ruins of the Philistine city of Ashkelon.

However, for the true people of God who trust in him, the day of the Lord is a time of wonderful blessing and restoration.

Outline

- Judgment: the day of the Lord (1:1–2:3)
- Judgment on the nations (2:4–15)
- Judgment on Jerusalem (3:1–8)
- Restoration of Jerusalem and the nations (3:9–13)
- Rejoicing in the Lord's salvation (3:14–20)

Interesting Features

- Zephaniah is called the "son of Cushi," implying some kind of connection to ancient Cush in Africa.
- The "day of the LORD" is a central theme of Zephaniah.
- Zephaniah preached salvation for all of the peoples of the earth.
- Zephaniah declares that God sings when he rejoices over his people.

Connections

Like the other prophets, Zephaniah sweeps away all superficial piety and unambiguously declares that arrogant, defiant, and rebellious people who ignore God's call and reject his message can expect to experience severe judgment from God. The prophets are not unclear on this point. Sin is serious business; God does not merely look the other way or ignore it. On the other hand, Zephaniah proclaims a message that foreshadows the gospel. God provides a way of salvation for those who humbly and obediently seek him and listen to his message.

Another interesting application is that Zephaniah's message can help us to know God better. Many people picture God as somber and cold, a scowling old man with a beard, sitting on a throne. Zephaniah pictures God as singing and rejoicing over those who are saved. Though we might anticipate that when we see God for the first time, he will be seated on a high throne, perhaps looking at us sternly, Zephaniah introduces the idea that God might be overflowing with excitement and joy to the extent that he breaks out in a joyful song!

Haggai

Rebuilding the Temple

Central Teaching

Haggai exhorts the returned exiles in Jerusalem to put aside selfish attitudes and to rebuild the temple of God.

Memory Verse

Is it a time for you yourselves to be living in your paneled houses, while this house remains a ruin? (Hag. 1:4)

Setting

Haggai was a prophet living in Jerusalem during the postexilic time, delivering the words of his prophecy in 520 BC. The Israelite exiles had recently returned from Babylon and were beginning to rebuild the city of Jerusalem. Throughout the book, the continued reference to the reign of Persian kings (1:1, 15; 2:10) reminds the reader that the Persians still dominated the area and that Davidic kings did not sit on the throne in Jerusalem.

Message

Many of the Israelite exiles returned to Israel after the Persian king Cyrus decreed that such peoples could go back to their lands. But such a return was difficult. Resources were scarce and these former exiles were not wealthy. While many of them resettled in Jerusalem and began to rebuild the society and the commercial structure there, the people became so focused on their own personal well-being that they neglected to keep their focus on God. They abandoned any idea of rebuilding God's temple, thus relegating the worship of God to the fringes of their concerns. Haggai, however, confronts them over this marginalization of God and convinces them to focus again on worshiping God. Step one, Haggai proclaims, is to rebuild the temple, which is the major theme of Haggai.

The people work energetically on rebuilding the temple, but they simply do not have the resources to build an impressive building, much less a spectacular structure such as their forefather Solomon built. As a result, they are disappointed in their new temple. God, however, does not seem to be bothered by this, and he exhorts them to be strong and continue the work, restating that "I am with you" (2:4). The presence of God among them is more important than the splendor of the stones in the physical temple structure. In 2:9 the Lord declares, "The glory of this present house will be greater than the glory of the former house." This is a surprising statement, especially when one compares the rebuilt structure

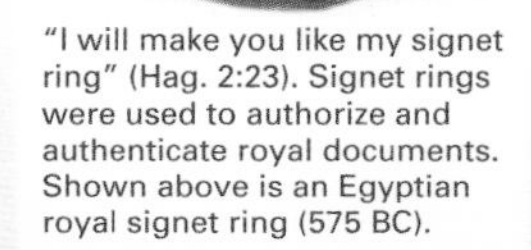

"I will make you like my signet ring" (Hag. 2:23). Signet rings were used to authorize and authenticate royal documents. Shown above is an Egyptian royal signet ring (575 BC).

A model of the Second Temple in the time of Herod

with the spectacular grandeur of the Solomonic temple. God's promise finds fulfillment, however, when Jesus Christ enters this temple 550 years later, bringing such glory with him that it overshadows the glory of the Solomonic temple, even with all of its gold and splendor.

Outline

- The call to rebuild the temple (1:1–15)
- The future glory of the temple (2:1–9)
- Moving from defiled to blessed (2:10–19)
- Restoration through the Lord's ruler (2:20–23)

Interesting Features

- The book of Haggai stresses the continued Persian domination.
- Haggai focuses on rebuilding the temple.
- Haggai speaks of the future glory (Christ) that will come to this temple.

Connections

For many of us in the church today, Haggai nails us right between the eyes. Haggai points out to the people of Jerusalem that they have their priorities mixed up; they are more concerned with their own houses than with the worship of God. Does this apply to us today? Most certainly. We spend more time and money on ourselves, often giving to the Lord our meager leftovers, if even that. Haggai tells us to make serving and worshiping the Lord our top priority in everything, including our budgets.

Zechariah

Looking to the Future

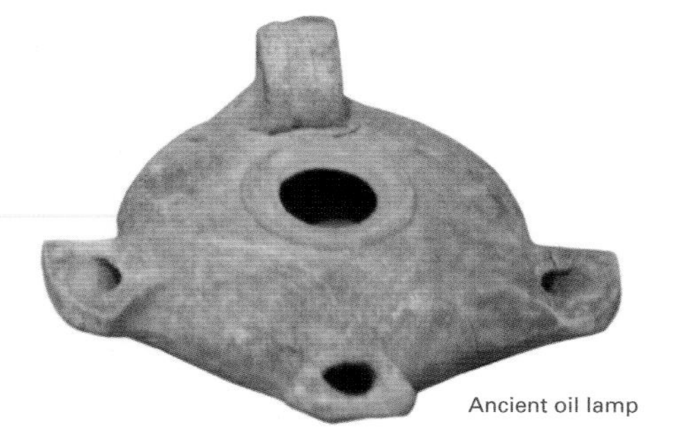
Ancient oil lamp

Central Teaching

Zechariah encourages the returned exiles to rebuild the temple and to keep their hope faithfully focused on the coming Messiah.

Memory Verse

"Not by might nor by power, but by my Spirit," says the LORD Almighty. (Zech. 4:6)

Setting

Zechariah provides us with several precise dates for his ministry, all connected to the reign of Darius, the powerful king of Persia. These dates place Zechariah's ministry in the years 520–518 BC and make him a contemporary of Haggai. Thus Zechariah speaks to the postexilic situation. The terrible judgment predicted by the preexilic prophets (the Babylonian invasion, the destruction of Jerusalem, and the exile) has come and gone. At least some of the Israelites are back in the land, trying to reestablish the shattered nation. Zechariah's frequent mention of the Persian king Darius is a reminder that the postexilic situation is not the glorious restoration that was promised by Isaiah, Jeremiah, and the rest of the preexilic prophets; that restoration will be

In Zechariah 4 the prophet describes a vision involving two olive trees. Olive trees still grow today throughout the Middle East.

characterized by a powerful Davidic king ruling over Israel with all other nations in subordination.

Like Ezekiel, Zechariah was probably a priest. His name means "the Lord remembers," which fits very well with the message of the book.

Message

While most of the prophets stress covenant violation and judgment, Zechariah focuses more on the future, when the Messiah will come and gloriously restore his people (and the nations) to relationship with him. Like Haggai, Zechariah is very concerned with the rebuilding of the temple, but like Ezekiel, Zechariah also points to something bigger and more spectacular beyond the physical temple they are building. Intertwined into this future vision is the presence of God, a constant theme in the prophetic books.

Like many of the other prophetic books, Zechariah addresses the foreign nations. He proclaims judgment on them for their sinful actions but also includes them in his picture of the glorious future, when they will come streaming to Jerusalem to worship God.

Outline

- Visions, justice, and restoration (1–8)
  - The introductory call to repentance (1:1–6)
  - Eight visions (1:7–6:8)
  - A symbolic crowning of the high priest (6:9–15)
  - A call to live by justice (7:1–14)
  - Future restoration (8:1–23)
- The coming Messiah (9–14)
  - Oracle 1: the advent and rejection of the Coming One (9:1–11:17)
  - Oracle 2: the advent and acceptance of the Coming One (12:1–14:21)

A modern-day Middle Eastern donkey

Interesting Features

- Zechariah contains some very unusual visions (such as a flying scroll and a woman in a basket).
- Many of the visions and images in the book of Revelation are connected to Zechariah.
- Zechariah describes the Coming King as riding into Jerusalem on a donkey.
- Zechariah is told that God's Spirit will empower those who carry out God's plan.

Connections

Zechariah is filled with numerous prophetic references to the Messiah—prophecies that were fulfilled by Jesus Christ. This should help to convince us, beyond a shadow of a doubt, that Jesus is indeed the Messiah who was promised by God through the Old Testament prophets. Zechariah also gives us numerous guidelines for our day-to-day lives. He points out that the important accomplishments of life are not achieved by human might or power but by God's Spirit. Zechariah reminds us of the close association between God's holiness, his presence, and his power made available to us. In addition, Zechariah echoes the ever-present prophetic theme of social justice, admonishing us: "Administer true justice; show mercy and compassion to one another. Do not oppress the widow or the fatherless, the foreigner or the poor" (7:9–10).

Malachi

Worship Faithfully and Wait Expectantly

Central Teaching

The returned exiles in Judah should worship God faithfully while expectantly waiting for the time of restoration.

Memory Verse

> *See, I will send the prophet Elijah to you before that great and dreadful day of the LORD comes. (Mal. 4:5)*

Setting

The name Malachi means "my messenger." Unlike Haggai, Malachi does not contain any historical superscriptions that tie his ministry to the reign of a certain king. Thus it is difficult to date Malachi with precision. However, the situation that Malachi appears to address in his book seems very similar to the situation that Nehemiah encountered. If Malachi was indeed a contemporary of Nehemiah, then the setting for this book is around 430 BC, ninety years after Haggai and Zechariah.

Message

Malachi addresses the postexilic community—those Israelites who returned to Jerusalem and the surrounding areas after the Babylonian captivity. Some may have thought that this return was the great and glorious restoration that the earlier prophets predicted, but the postexilic prophets (Malachi, Haggai, Zechariah) disagree and remind everyone that the great day of the Lord is still to come, even though the return of the exiles could be viewed as the early beginnings of God's unfolding plan of restoration.

Ornate incense shovels like these were often used in temple worship to remove ash from incense burners. Malachi rebukes the priests of Jerusalem for corrupt, hypocritical, ritualistic worship.

Malachi is particularly concerned with how Israel will live and worship God in the meantime, as they await the coming day of the Lord. He speaks strongly against the corrupt forms of worship and day-to-day living that are occurring in his time—unacceptable sacrifices, corrupt priests, refusal to tithe and to support the temple, and social injustice.

Outline

- Dialogue 1: the Lord's love for Israel (1:1–5)
- Dialogue 2: the corruption of the priesthood (1:6–2:9)
- Dialogue 3: unfaithfulness—divorce and marrying pagans (2:10–16)
- Dialogue 4: When will God bring justice? (2:17–3:5)
- Dialogue 5: Will you rob God? (3:6–12)
- Dialogue 6: deliverance for the righteous, judgment for the wicked (3:13–4:3)
- Conclusion: obey and wait (4:4–6)

While Israel waits for the Messiah, they are to obey the laws and teaching (Torah) that God gave to Moses at Mount Horeb (Mount Sinai).

Interesting Features

- Malachi ends the Book of the Twelve (the Minor Prophets) with the same theme that began it—the love of God for his people.
- Malachi is structured around six dialogues (or disagreements) between God and his people.
- Malachi prophesies that Elijah will come again, signaling the inauguration of the day of the Lord.
- Malachi contains some of the strongest language against divorce in the Old Testament (2:10–16).
- In Malachi, God accuses Israel of "robbing God" (3:8) because they did not tithe.

Connections

There are a lot of great applications for us from the short book of Malachi. We can see how important it is to worship God truthfully, with a sincere heart, rather than ritually or hypocritically. Likewise, Malachi reminds us that failing to support the true worship of God is a form of robbery. If we fail to tithe to our local churches, selfishly keeping this money for ourselves, we are not worshiping God sincerely; indeed, we are stealing from him.

The book of Malachi also adds to the witness of the other biblical books concerning God's intention for marriage—that both husband and wife stay faithful to each other. Furthermore, Malachi exhorts us to marry within the faith.

Finally, Malachi gives us encouragement to continue to look expectantly toward the future. We should not be discouraged or become cynical just because the wicked are flourishing for a short while. We should trust in God's word through the prophets; he is working to bring about his kingdom and to establish justice throughout the world. When the Lord returns, all things will be brought under his rule. Justice will be established, and God's people will be blessed beyond imagination.

Old Testament Messianic Prophecies

The entire Old Testament story points to a future time when God will send a messianic king to restore all things and to make salvation available for all who will accept it. Thus the coming of Jesus Christ in the New Testament is the culmination of the entire Old Testament. When placed in the context of the bigger story, everything in the Old Testament points to Christ.

Yet while all of the stories, themes, and prophecies in the Old Testament generally and collectively point to Christ, numerous prophecies within the Old Testament specifically prophesy details about Jesus, the Coming One. Not all of them can be presented here, but we have listed a few of the more significant ones below.

The Messiah will be from the tribe of Judah. "The scepter will not depart from Judah, nor the ruler's staff from between his feet, until he to whom it belongs shall come and the obedience of the nations shall be his" (Gen. 49:10; Matt. 1:1–3).

The Messiah will be born in the town of Bethlehem. "But you Bethlehem Ephrathah, though you are small among the clans of Judah, out of you will come for me one who will be ruler over Israel, whose origins are from of old, from ancient times" (Mic. 5:2; Matt. 2:1–6).

The Messiah will be a very special child, born of a virgin and called "God with us" (Immanuel); he will reign on the throne of David. "Therefore, the Lord himself will give you a sign: The virgin will conceive and give birth to a son, and will call him Immanuel. . . . For to us a child is born, to us a son is given, and the government will be on his shoulders. And he will be called Wonderful Counselor, Mighty God, Everlasting Father, Prince of Peace. Of the greatness of his government and peace there will be no end. He will reign on David's throne and over his kingdom, establishing and upholding it with justice and righteousness from that time on and forever" (Isa. 7:14; 9:6–7; Matt. 1:18–23).

The Messiah will be preceded by a special prophetic messenger (John the Baptist). "A voice of one calling: 'In the wilderness prepare the way for the Lord; make straight in the desert a highway for our God. Every valley shall be raised up, every mountain and hill made low; the rough ground shall become level, the rugged places a plain. And the glory of the Lord will be revealed, and all people will see it together.'

For the mouth of the LORD has spoken" (Isa. 40:3–5; Matt. 3:1–3).

The Messiah will not only restore the remnant of Israel but also be a light for the Gentiles (non-Jews). "It is too small a thing for you to be my servant to restore the tribes of Jacob and bring back those of Israel I have kept. I will also make you a light for the Gentiles, that my salvation may reach to the ends of the earth" (Isa. 49:6; Luke 2:25–32; John 1:4–9; Acts 13:47).

The Messiah will bring good news to the poor and the oppressed. "The Spirit of the Sovereign LORD is on me, because the LORD has anointed me to proclaim good news to the poor. He has sent me to bind up the brokenhearted, to proclaim freedom for the captives and release from darkness for the prisoners . . . to comfort all who mourn" (Isa. 61:1–2; Luke 4:18–19).

The Messiah will care for his people like a good shepherd. "I myself will search for my sheep and look after them. As a shepherd looks after his scattered flock when he is with them, so will I look after my sheep. I will rescue them. . . . I will bring them out. . . . I will pasture them. . . . I will tend them. . . . I will search for the lost and bring back the strays. . . . I will place over them one shepherd, my servant David, and he will tend them; he will tend them and be their shepherd" (Ezek. 34:11–14, 16, 23; John 10:1–30).

The Messiah will give his life as a substitute for the people he saves. "Surely he took up our pain and bore our suffering. . . . But he was pierced for our transgressions, he was crushed for our iniquities; the punishment that brought us peace was on him, and by his wounds we are healed. We all, like sheep, have gone astray, each of us has turned to our own way; and the LORD has laid on him the iniquity of us all" (Isa. 53:4–6; Mark 10:45; Rom. 3:23–25).

The Messiah will be called the "Son of Man" and will return with the clouds of heaven. "Before me was one like a son of man, coming with the clouds of heaven. . . . He was given authority, glory and sovereign power; all nations and peoples of every language worshiped him" (Dan. 7:13–14; Matt. 24:30–31; Mark 13:26–27; Luke 21:27).

Between the Testaments

The time between the Old and the New Testaments covers roughly four hundred years, beginning in about 430 BC.[1] During this period, the world's power shifted from Asia to Europe. The Persian Empire collapsed under the attacks of the Macedonians, and the Greek Empire eventually gave way to Roman rule.

The Persian period extends from the end of the Old Testament story to 334 BC. In 539 BC Cyrus of Persia conquered Babylon and began to rule over its territories. Cyrus's empire spread from Greece to India and from the Caucasus to Egypt, during which time Cyrus allowed the Jews to return to Judea and rebuild their temple and city. The Persian rule of Palestine was generally tolerant. During the fourth century BC, Cyrus's Persian Empire began to crumble, and European power moved into Palestine.

Philip II of Macedon began a new period in the history of Palestine after uniting the city-states of Greece and Macedonia. Philip's son, Alexander III ("the Great"), defeated Persia in battle, thus combining Egypt, Palestine, Syria, Asia Minor, Greece, and the Persian territory into an extensive empire. The expanded empire was administered following principles of the Greek *polis* (city-state), with Greece forming new cities and reshaping existing cities. This process of blending Greek culture with native cultures (known as "Hellenization") continued throughout the intertestamental period.

Silver coin with the head of Alexander the Great

After Alexander's death in 323 BC, his empire was divided among his four generals, the Diadochi ("successors"). Most significant to Palestine were Ptolemy I, whose forces held Egypt and North Africa, and Seleucus Nicator (Seleucus I), whose armies secured Syria, Asia Minor, and Babylonia.

The Ptolemaic kings governed Palestine from 323 to 198 BC, allowing the Jews to govern themselves and observe their religious customs. In 198 BC, Antiochus III, ruler of the Seleucids, defeated his Ptolemaic rival and annexed Palestine, continuing the Ptolemies' policy of religious toleration.

1. Much of this article is taken from James L. Johns's article on the intertestamental period in the *Baker Illustrated Bible Handbook* (Grand Rapids: Baker Books, 2011), 465–68.

In 175 BC, however, Antiochus IV "Epiphanes" ("the manifest god") came to power, which began the most significant crisis of Second Temple Judaism before Pompey's invasion and the onset of Roman rule. Along with others in Jerusalem, Antiochus IV supported the radical Hellenization of Jerusalem. He outlawed Judaism, made pagan worship practices compulsory, and brought in foreign mercenaries to maintain order. An altar to the Syrian god Zeus was erected in the temple. By 167 BC, animals forbidden by Mosaic law were sacrificed on the altar, and prostitution was sanctioned in the temple precincts.

The Hasmoneans, a priestly family named after one of their ancestors and consisting of a man named Mattathias and his five sons, raised a revolt that proved successful after an intense struggle (this family was also called Maccabees, from the nickname "Maccabeus" or "the Hammer," which was given to Judas, one of Mattathias's sons). Judas Maccabeus and his revolutionaries defeated the Syrians and recaptured the temple in 164 BC. However, the Hasmonean dynasty deteriorated through weak leadership because the political aims of the Hasmoneans alienated many former supporters, including the Hasideans, who split into the Pharisees and the Essenes. The aristocratic supporters of the Hasmonean priest-kings became the Sadducees. Toward the end of the Hasmonean dynasty the Pharisees dominated the country. In 67 BC, a war broke out between two brothers, Hyracanus II and Aristobulus II, each fighting for the title of high priest and king. Both appealed to Rome to settle the issue, effectively inviting the Roman general Pompey to conquer Jerusalem in 63 BC and bring Judea under direct Roman control.

Alexander the Great fulfills the prophecy of Daniel 8.

Under its emperors, Roman culture remained largely Hellenistic, with the distinctive Roman contributions of central administration and the promise of peace through superior force. Pompey, the Roman general who seized control of Jerusalem and the surrounding area, delegated much of the former Hasmonean territory to the nearby Roman governor of Syria. After conferring the title of high priest on Hyracanus II, Pompey appointed an Idumean (a descendant of Esau) named Antipater and his sons, Phasel and Herod, as governors of Judea and Galilee. Hyracanus II's years of limited religious rule ended with defeat by the Parthians. In turn, Rome defeated the Parthians and then confirmed Herod ("the Great") as ruler in 37 BC.

During these early years of Roman control, Rome was generally quite tolerant of Judaism. In addition, Roman power provided a period of relative peace for the region. However, throughout the period of Roman domination, sporadic Jewish resistance movements emerged. Herod was an efficient ruler and a clever politician who kept Rome satisfied. Among his many building projects, perhaps his greatest contribution was the expansion and beautification of the temple in Jerusalem. Herod is also known for promoting Hellenistic (Greek) culture throughout his realm. Herod's reign was filled with internal political intrigue, plots, murders, wars, and brutality until his death in 4 BC. Lacking their father's ability and ambition, Herod's sons ruled over separate parts of Palestine into the New Testament period.

The New Testament

An Overview

The New Testament was originally written in Greek, the common language of much of the Roman Empire during the first century AD. The main concern of the New Testament is the covenant established by the life, death, and resurrection of Jesus Christ and the people who embrace that covenant, the church. Historically, the entire New Testament period covers less than one hundred years, and the writings of the New Testament include the Gospels, the book of Acts, Paul's Letters, the General Letters, and the book of Revelation.

The Four Gospels

The four Gospels—Matthew, Mark, Luke, and John—tell the story of Jesus Christ. The English word "gospel" comes from the Greek word *euangelion,* which means "good news." These four books tell the good news of salvation that God has provided in Jesus Christ through his powerful ministry, his atoning death, and his miraculous resurrection. While the term "gospel" refers to the message about Jesus, it came to be used to refer to the written accounts of this message—the four Gospels. The first three Gospels are known as the Synoptic Gospels because they can be placed side-by-side and "seen together" (syn-optic), while the Gospel of John follows a slightly different chronology in presenting the story of Jesus.

The Book of Acts

There are four versions of the life of Jesus (the Gospels), but only one account of the life of the early church—the book of Acts. The term "acts" refers to the acts of the Holy Spirit through the apostles and other Christians. The book of Acts tells the story of the birth and growth of the early church from about AD 30 to the early 60s.

Paul's Letters

Traditionally, the apostle Paul is credited with writing thirteen letters that are included in the Bible. These letters may be organized into four groups: early letters (Galatians, 1–2 Thessalonians), major letters (Romans, 1–2 Corinthians), prison letters (Ephesians, Philippians, Colossians, Philemon), and Pastoral Epistles (1–2 Timothy, Titus). In the Bible, Paul's Letters are arranged according to length, from the longest (Romans) to the shortest (Philemon).

The General Letters

James, 1–2 Peter, 1–3 John, Jude, and sometimes Hebrews are often called the General or Catholic Letters (meaning "universal") for a simple reason: each takes its title from the author of the letter and not from the people receiving it. In contrast to Paul's Letters, which are addressed to more specific groups (i.e., to the Philippians or to the Colossians), the General Letters are addressed to more general audiences. Often 1–3 John are referred to as the Johannine Letters.

Because Hebrews takes its name from the audience (as in the case of Paul's Letters) rather than the author, some do not include Hebrews with the General Letters.

Revelation

The final book of the New Testament depicts God's ultimate victory over the forces of evil. The title "Revelation" comes from the Greek word *apocalypsis*, meaning "revelation" or "unveiling." The book is a "revelation of Jesus Christ" (Rev. 1:1 HCSB), suggesting that the book reveals something about Jesus or that Jesus reveals something about God's plan or perhaps both. Revelation differs from the other New Testament books in that it integrates three different literary types: letter, prophecy, and apocalyptic.

New Testament Time Line

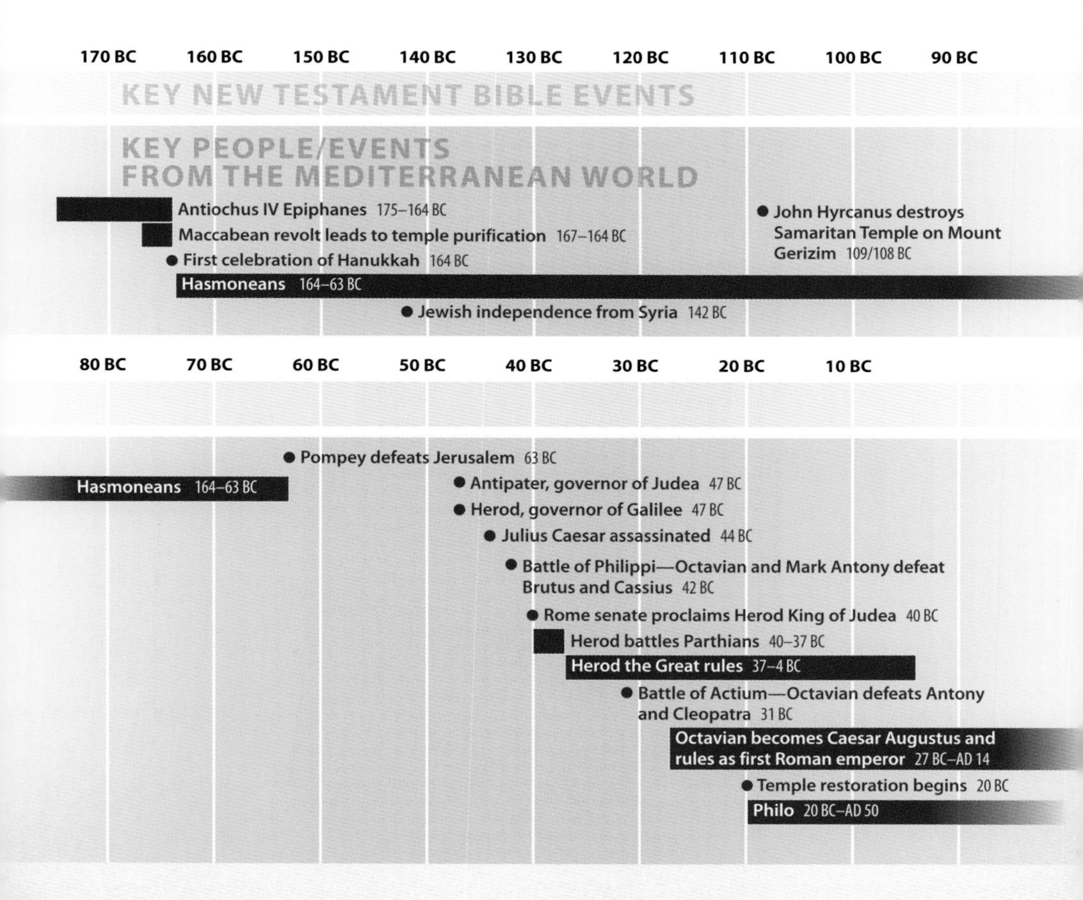

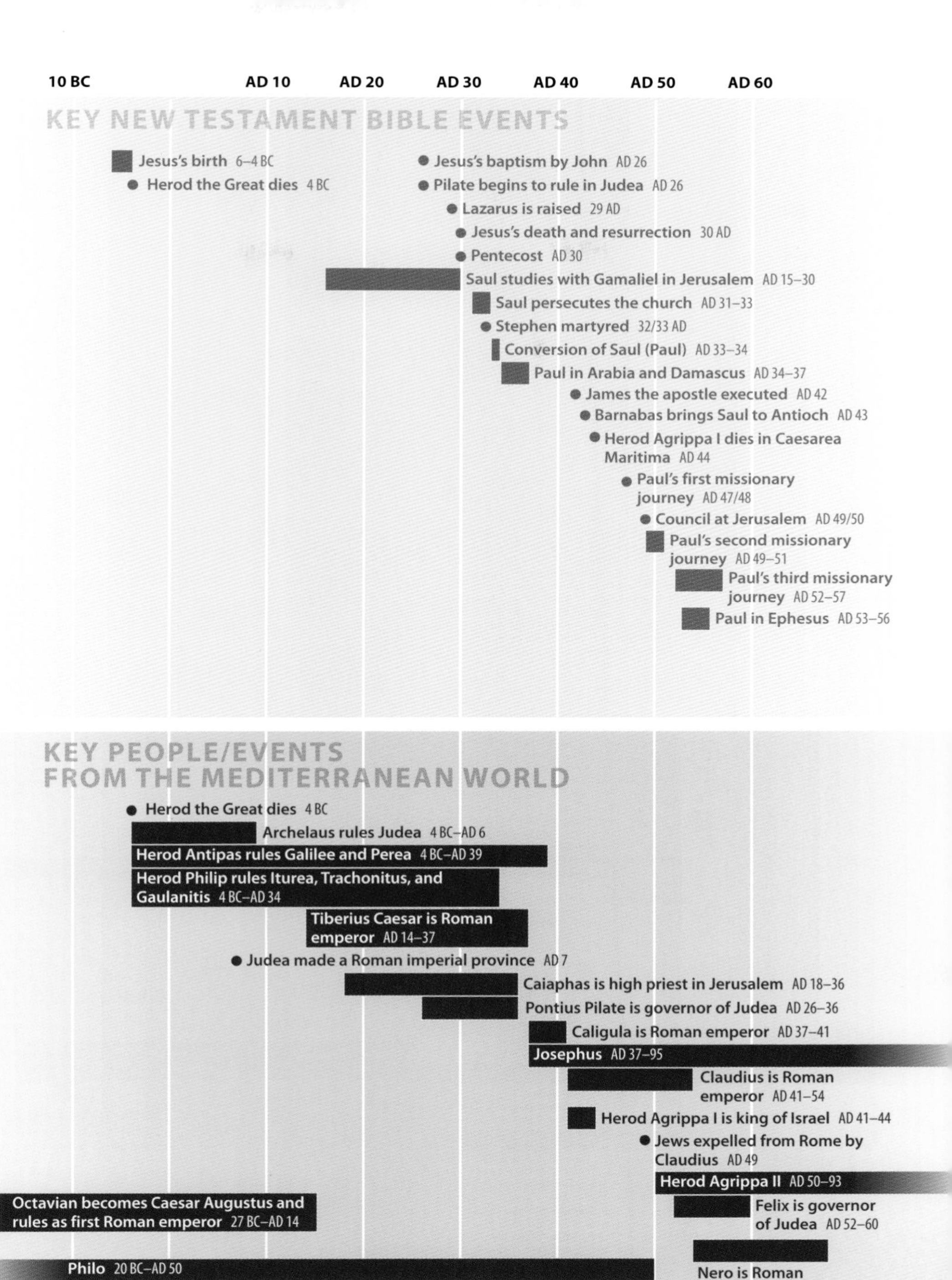

10 BC
AD 10
AD 20
AD 30
AD 40
AD 50
AD 60
KEY NEW TESTAMENT BIBLE EVENTS
Jesus's birth 6–4 BC
Herod the Great dies 4 BC
Jesus's baptism by John AD 26
Pilate begins to rule in Judea AD 26
Lazarus is raised 29 AD
Jesus's death and resurrection 30 AD
Pentecost AD 30
Saul studies with Gamaliel in Jerusalem AD 15–30
Saul persecutes the church AD 31–33
Stephen martyred 32/33 AD
Conversion of Saul (Paul) AD 33–34
Paul in Arabia and Damascus AD 34–37
James the apostle executed AD 42
Barnabas brings Saul to Antioch AD 43
Herod Agrippa I dies in Caesarea Maritima AD 44
Paul's first missionary journey AD 47/48
Council at Jerusalem AD 49/50
Paul's second missionary journey AD 49–51
Paul's third missionary journey AD 52–57
Paul in Ephesus AD 53–56
KEY PEOPLE/EVENTS FROM THE MEDITERRANEAN WORLD
Herod the Great dies 4 BC
Archelaus rules Judea 4 BC–AD 6
Herod Antipas rules Galilee and Perea 4 BC–AD 39
Herod Philip rules Iturea, Trachonitus, and Gaulanitis 4 BC–AD 34
Tiberius Caesar is Roman emperor AD 14–37
Judea made a Roman imperial province AD 7
Caiaphas is high priest in Jerusalem AD 18–36
Pontius Pilate is governor of Judea AD 26–36
Caligula is Roman emperor AD 37–41
Josephus AD 37–95
Claudius is Roman emperor AD 41–54
Herod Agrippa I is king of Israel AD 41–44
Jews expelled from Rome by Claudius AD 49
Herod Agrippa II AD 50–93
Octavian becomes Caesar Augustus and rules as first Roman emperor 27 BC–AD 14
Felix is governor of Judea AD 52–60
Philo 20 BC–AD 50
Nero is Roman emperor AD 54–68
10 BC
AD 10
AD 20
AD 30
AD 40
AD 50
AD 60

AD 60 AD 70 AD 80 AD 90 AD 100 AD 110 AD 120 AD 130 AD 140

KEY NEW TESTAMENT BIBLE EVENTS

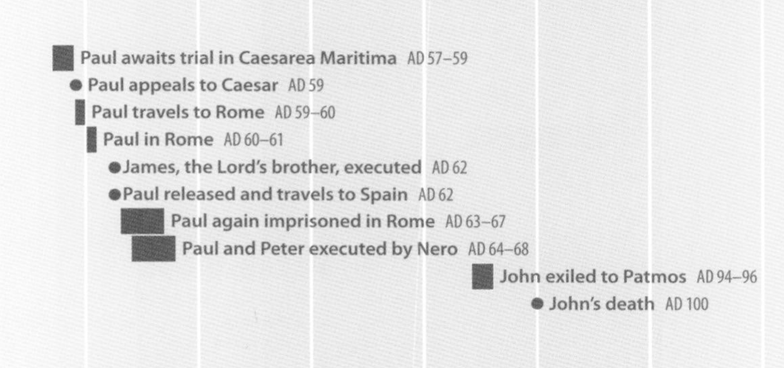

KEY PEOPLE/EVENTS FROM THE MEDITERRANEAN WORLD

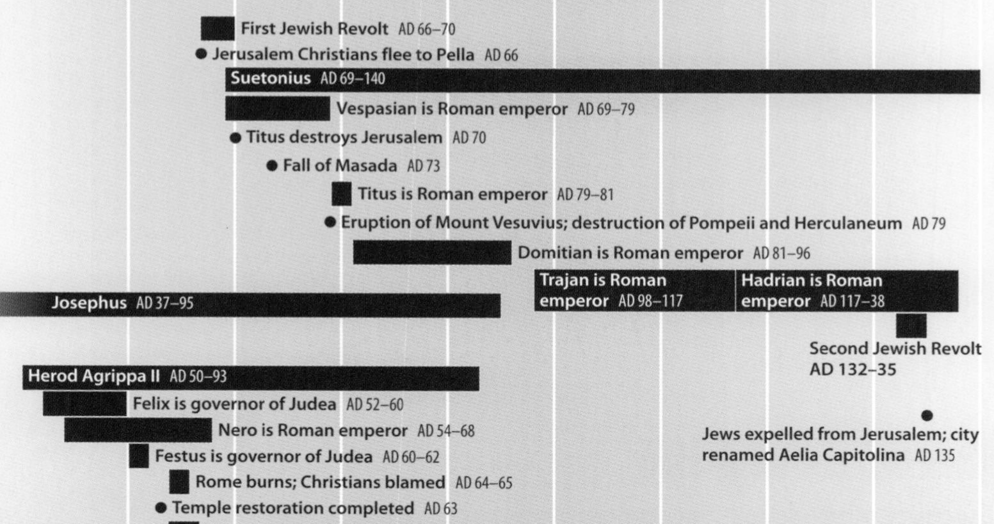

AD 60 AD 70 AD 80 AD 90 AD 100 AD 110 AD 120 AD 130 AD 140

New Testament Maps

Jerusalem in the Time of the New Testament

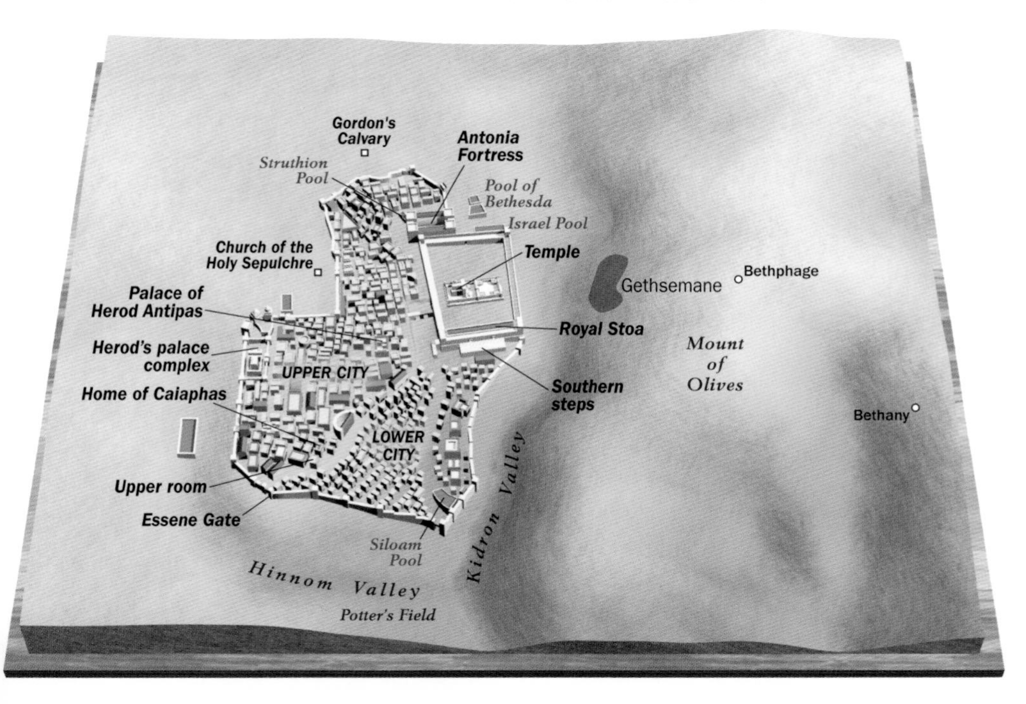

Palestine in the Time of the New Testament

Paul's Missionary Journeys

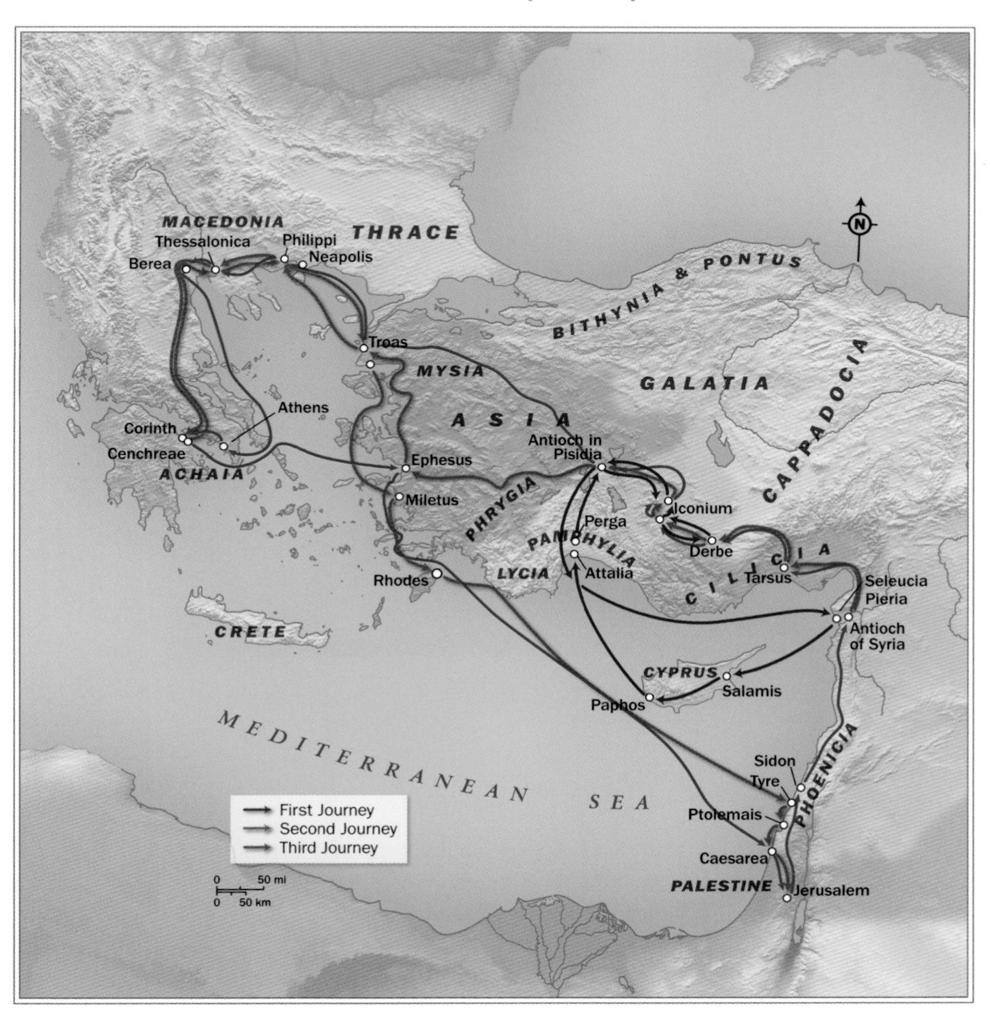

The Roman World

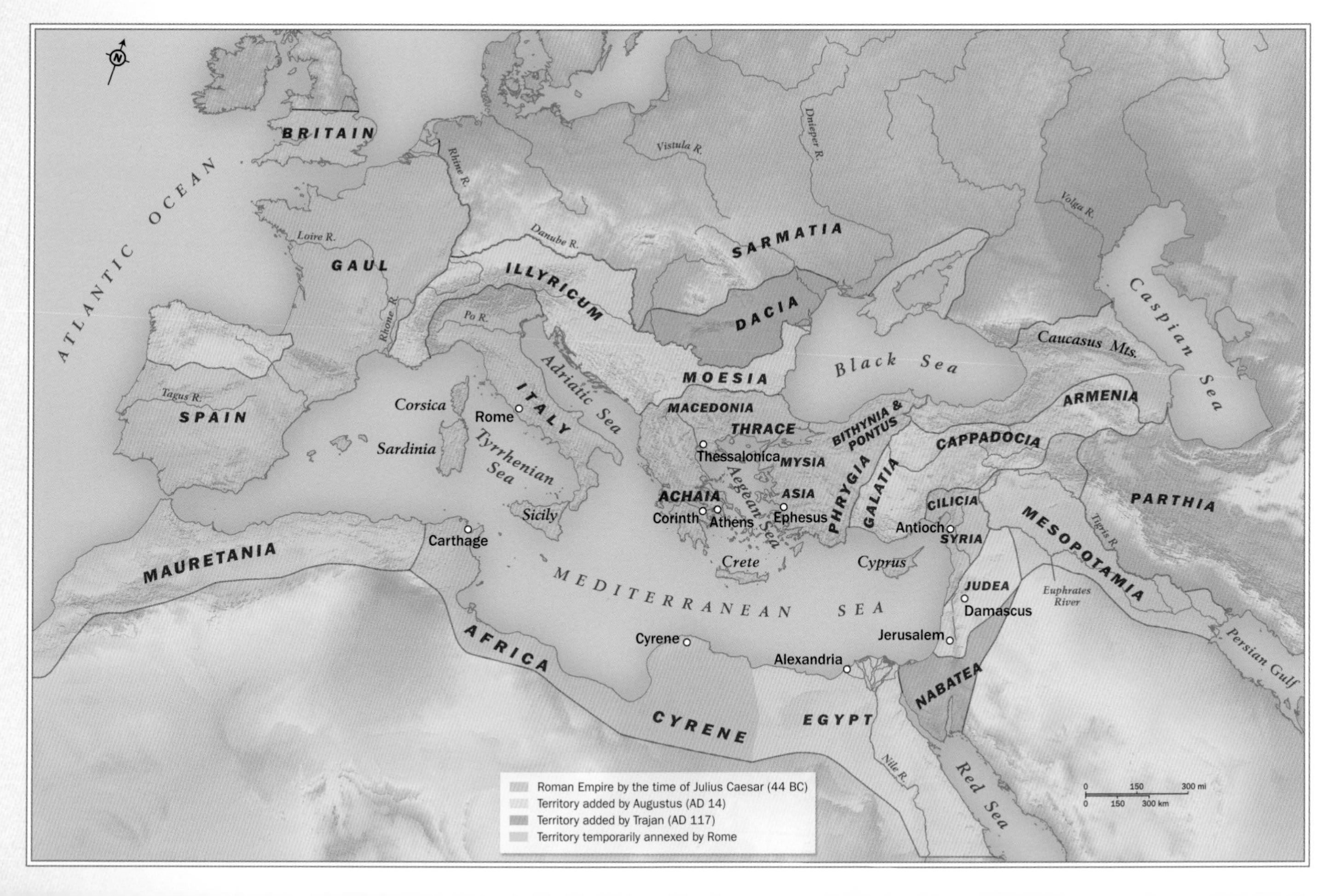

The New Testament Book by Book

Matthew

Jesus, the Jewish Messiah, Brings Salvation to the Whole World

A portion of Papyrus 37, a New Testament manuscript of the Gospel of Matthew

Central Teaching

Jesus, the true King and Jewish Messiah, fulfills God's plan to save his people from their sins and bring salvation to the nations.

Memory Verses

> ***All authority in heaven and on earth has been given to me. Therefore go and make disciples of all nations, baptizing them in the name of the Father and of the Son and of the Holy Spirit, and teaching them to obey everything I have commanded you. And surely I am with you always. (Matt. 28:18–20)***

Setting

This Gospel was written by Matthew/Levi, the tax collector who became a disciple of Jesus (9:9–13; 10:3). Matthew seems to rely on Mark's Gospel (the testimony of the apostle Peter), and Matthew probably wrote his Gospel shortly after Mark composed his own, which can be dated to the early AD 60s. Matthew is the most Jewish of the four Gospels and has significant parallels with the letter of James, another early Jewish-Christian document. Matthew is writing for a Jewish-Christian community (or at least a mixed community of Jewish and Gentile Christians) that is in the process of breaking with Judaism. He wants to show that Jesus is the long-awaited Jewish Messiah who fulfills God's promises to Israel.

A mosaic of loaves and fishes in the church at Tabgha

Message

Matthew's main concern is to show that Jesus is the true King and Messiah, sent to save the Jewish people from their sins but also to bring God's salvation to the nations. Jesus is "the Messiah [Christ], the son of David, the son of Abraham" (1:1). This new movement within Judaism (eventually identified as Christianity) is the authentic Judaism because Jesus is the true Messiah. Matthew uses five discourses (perhaps reminding readers of the first five books of the Old Testament and depicting Jesus as the new Moses), followed by additional teaching sections. Thus, Matthew explains how Jesus fulfills the Old Testament law and prophets in bringing salvation to humanity. Jesus teaches his disciples how to live as kingdom citizens (Matt. 5–7), how to carry out

The Church of the Beatitudes in Tabgha along the Sea of Galilee

the kingdom mission (Matt. 10), how to be loyal to God's kingdom while living in an earthly kingdom (Matt. 13), how to live in community (Matt. 18), and how to stay faithful until the King returns to consummate his kingdom (Matt. 23–25).

Outline

- Introduction and preparation for public ministry (1:1–4:25)
- Discourse 1—Sermon on the Mount (5:1–7:29)
- Jesus's messianic authority (8:1–9:38)
- Discourse 2—The mission of the Messiah (10:1–42)
- Opposition to Jesus the Messiah and his mission (11:1–12:50)
- Discourse 3—parables of the kingdom (13:1–52)
- Jesus's identity as the crucified and risen Messiah (13:53–17:27)
- Discourse 4—the community of the Messiah (18:1–35)
- Jesus teaches on true and false discipleship (19:1–23:39)
- Discourse 5—the Olivet discourse (24:1–25:46)
- Jesus's crucifixion, resurrection, and Great Commission (26:1–28:20)

Interesting Features

- The book of Matthew features the Sermon on the Mount (5–7), which includes many of Jesus's most famous teachings.
- Matthew highlights Jesus as the Teacher and organizes his teaching into five long teaching discourses.
- The book of Matthew uses the uncommon phrase "kingdom of heaven" and is the only Gospel to mention the "church" directly (16:16–20; 18:15–20).

Connections

Matthew reminds us that Jesus the Messiah came to rescue us from sin. He came to set us free. Through Jesus's teachings we can find profound direction and abundant wisdom for our walk with God. Jesus is also depicted as powerful and authoritative, casting out demons, healing, showing compassion, forgiving sins, and judging evil. Sometimes we forget that Jesus has power to actually change our lives. Rather than trusting our ingenuity and abilities, we should submit to the King and trust him to work. Jesus speaks often about how Christians should treat one another (e.g., forgiving each other, Matt. 6:14–15). First and foremost, our faith should be evident in our families and communities.

Mark

Following Jesus, the Suffering Son of God

Central Teaching

Jesus, the powerful Messiah and Son of God, is also the Suffering Servant who died on the cross to save us from our sins.

Memory Verse

For even the Son of Man did not come to be served, but to serve, and to give his life as a ransom for many. (Mark 10:45)

An ancient oil lamp

Setting

Mark was probably written by John Mark, who is mentioned in other parts of the New Testament. Early Christian tradition tells us that Mark relied heavily on the preaching of Simon Peter as his primary source. In a real sense, the Gospel of Mark is Simon Peter's Gospel. Mark was likely in Rome with Peter during the AD 60s when the church was facing intense persecution under Emperor Nero. Mark writes primarily to encourage Gentile Christians in and around Rome to follow Jesus even when it means suffering as a disciple.

Message

Mark's main concern is to show that Jesus, the powerful Messiah and Son of God, is also the Suffering Servant. Notice how Mark's aim of showing Jesus as the Suffering Son of God encircles the entire Gospel:

Mark 1:1— The beginning of the good news about Jesus the Messiah, the Son of God.

Mark 15:39—"Surely this man was the Son of God!"

Between these bookends, Jesus shows what it means that he is the Son of God and Messiah (see especially Mark 8:28–29; 10:45). Mark then connects who Jesus is (Christology) to what it means to follow Jesus (discipleship). We learn that following Jesus means going the way of the cross—that the path to glory leads through suffering, not only for the Lord but also for those who follow him. Mark's first readers, who were navigating the turbulent waters of persecution, needed this message. Jesus the Son

A tomb with a rolling stone

The synagogue at Capernaum. The light stone structure dates to after the time of Christ but rests on the remains of a synagogue dating to the first century (dark stone).

of God reigns supreme over every evil power, but the greatest demonstration of his power comes at the cross, where he gives his life as a ransom for many (10:45).

Outline

- Preparation and beginning of Jesus's public ministry (1:1–45)
- Ministry of divine power rejected by the religious leaders (2:1–3:6)
- Ministry of divine power rejected by Jesus's own people (3:7–6:6a)
- Jesus's ministry beyond Galilee (6:6b–8:21)
- Jesus's journey to Jerusalem (8:22–10:52)
- Jesus confronts Jerusalem (11:1–13:37)
- The suffering, death, and resurrection of Jesus, the Son of God (14:1–16:8)

Interesting Features

- Mark is a fast-moving, action-packed story of Jesus, the Son of God and Messiah, who conquers Satan, demons, sin, disease, death, and false religion.
- Mark focuses on Jesus's actions, especially his miracles, and shows how Jesus has come to liberate the world from the domain of evil and usher in the kingdom of God.
- Mark stresses the cross of Christ and the demands of discipleship (e.g., 8:34–38; 9:35–37; 10:42–45).

Connections

If Jesus, the Suffering Son of God, used his power to serve people, how much more should we use our God-given power to serve? The pagans use power to control and manipulate, but we should use power to love and serve. We should use our gifts, influence, and authority to benefit and edify other people. Following Jesus is costly, especially in an atmosphere of opposition. Though we sometimes expect everyone to accept us and like us and praise us, that is not the typical experience for Jesus's followers. When we are ridiculed, slighted, or excluded because of our connection to Jesus, we should remember that persecution is a normal part of Christian discipleship. The Christian life consists of actions, not merely words. In a culture in which "Christian" words are plentiful and sometimes lose their power, a consistent Christian lifestyle always speaks loudly.

Luke

Jesus, the Savior for All People

A stone manger (Luke 2:7)

Central Teaching

Jesus, the Savior for all people, came to seek and save the lost.

Memory Verses

> ***But the angel said to them, "Do not be afraid. I bring you good news that will cause great joy for all the people. Today in the town of David a Savior has been born to you; he is the Messiah, the Lord." (Luke 2:10–11)***

Setting

Luke, the well-educated Gentile, physician, and co-missionary of the apostle Paul, wrote Luke-Acts as a single book in two volumes. Although not an eyewitness of the life of Jesus, Luke did careful research (1:1–4) and wrote an orderly account of Jesus's life and ministry for "most excellent Theophilus" (Luke 1:3; Acts 1:1). Theophilus was likely a believer with wealth and influence who may have helped finance the copying and distribution of Luke-Acts. Luke seems to be writing primarily for Gentile Christians, emphasizing the comprehensive work of God (e.g., tracing Jesus's ancestry beyond Abraham to Adam). Since Luke makes use of other sources (possibly Mark or Matthew), this Gospel was probably written in the early to mid-60s.

Message

In Luke-Acts, Luke explains the grand plan of God through Jesus Christ and his church. Luke writes to Theophilus and others like him so that they may know the certainty of the things they have been taught (1:4). In other words, Luke provides a discipleship manual for new believers coming from a pagan background and living in an indifferent or openly hostile culture. Luke wants

The Church of the Nativity in Bethlehem

his readers to know that their faith rests on the facts of history, which are reflected in eyewitness testimony. The Christian faith was not invented by a community far removed from these events. God really did step into history in the person of Jesus and offer salvation to all people.

Luke gives a thorough report of Jesus's birth and childhood to make sure we know that Jesus is God's unique Son. Through his mighty miracles and powerful teaching, Jesus brings God's salvation to the whole world. He is the Savior for all people—Jew and Gentile, rich and poor, men and women, religious and pagan. The central section of Luke features Jesus's single-minded journey to Jerusalem to die for the sins of the world.

Outline

- The birth of Jesus, the Savior (1:1–2:52)
- The Savior's preparation for public ministry (3:1–4:13)
- The Savior's Galilean ministry (4:14–9:50)
- The Savior's journey to Jerusalem (9:51–19:44)
- The Savior's ministry in Jerusalem (19:45–21:38)
- The Savior is betrayed, tried, and crucified (22:1–23:56)
- The resurrection and ascension of Jesus, the Savior for all people (24:1–53)

Interesting Features

- Luke is the Gospel for all people, including social outcasts, Gentiles, Samaritans, women, the poor, the sick, and sinners.
- The birth stories in the Gospel of Luke feature four famous hymns—the Magnificat (1:46–55), the Benedictus (1:68–79), the Gloria in Excelsis (2:14), and the Nunc Dimittis (2:29–32).
- Luke presents more of Jesus's parables than any other Gospel and contains many of his best-known parables (e.g., good Samaritan, prodigal son).

Connections

In Luke, we learn from Jesus what it means to show compassion to those our society often pushes aside. So often, Jesus reaches out to the underdogs who are being ignored by the powerful. No one is beyond the grace of God! Jesus emphasizes the importance of prayer and joy and gratitude. He also tells us that we can't live the Christian life in our own strength; we must depend on the power of the Holy Spirit. Like Jesus's necessary journey to Jerusalem, our path as his followers includes both a willingness to suffer and the hope of glory. Jesus *moved toward* Jerusalem to suffer for the sins of the world, and he empowers us to *move away* from Jerusalem with the best news ever—the world has a Savior!

Inside a typical Galilean home

John

Believing in Jesus, the Son Sent from the Father

Central Teaching

God the Father sent the Son into the world to give eternal life to those who believe in him.

Memory Verses

> ***For God so loved the world that he gave his one and only Son, that whoever believes in him shall not perish but have eternal life. For God did not send his Son into the world to condemn the world, but to save the world through him. (John 3:16–17)***

Setting

Early church tradition points to John, the son of Zebedee and one of the Twelve, as the author of this Gospel. John refers to himself as "the disciple whom Jesus loved" (13:23). He was an eyewitness of the life and ministry of Jesus and, along with Peter and James, was part of Jesus's inner circle.

John writes from Ephesus at a time when the church was facing increasing opposition from Judaism. The phrase "the Jews" occurs more than seventy times in John's Gospel to describe Jesus's opponents. Many scholars believe that John is writing in the late first century (from the mid-60s to mid-90s), primarily for Christians who had pulled away from the Jewish synagogue. Along with encouraging them to continue trusting Jesus in the midst of difficult circumstances, he also writes to call others to faith in Christ.

Message

About 90 percent of John's Gospel is not found in Matthew, Mark, or Luke. John's language is plain but his meaning is profound. The church father Augustine is often quoted as saying that "the Gospel of John is deep enough for an elephant to swim and shallow enough for a child not to drown." While the book of John is often given to children and new converts, scholars continue to wrestle with its theological message.

John states his purpose in 20:31: "But these are written that you may believe that Jesus is the Messiah, the Son of God, and that by believing you may have life in his name." The Gospel opens by identifying Jesus as the Word who was with God and was God but has now become a human being to bring us

Traditional tomb of Lazarus in Bethany

life (John 1:1–18). The central section of the Gospel is divided into two books: the Book of Signs (1:19–12:50) features seven miracles that identify Jesus and call people to faith, while the Book of Glory (13:1–20:31) focuses on the last week of Jesus's life, his glorification. The epilogue (21:1–25) describes Jesus's appearances to his disciples after the resurrection, his restoration of Peter, and a word about the author of the Gospel.

Jesus declares, "I am the true vine, and my Father is the gardener" (John 15:1).

Outline

- The prologue (1:1–18)
- The Book of Signs (1:19–12:50)
- The Book of Glory (13:1–20:31)
- The epilogue (21:1–25)

Interesting Features

- The Gospel of John includes seven "I am" sayings and at least six (and likely seven) miracles or signs that point to Jesus as the unique Son of God.
- Almost half of this Gospel (13–21) deals with the last week of Jesus's life—the week of his passion.
- Eternal life is both a present reality and a future hope.
- Many of Jesus's teachings occur in the form of lengthy conversations (e.g., with Nicodemus in John 3), heated debates (e.g., with Jews in John 7), and private teaching (e.g., his farewell discourse in John 13–17).

Connections

John's pattern of deep substance in plain words challenges us to avoid both overly technical Christian terminology and superficial, religious foolishness when communicating the story of Jesus. John also calls us to a correct understanding of Jesus Christ as the fully divine and fully human revelation of the Father; he is God incarnate. When we get confused about God, we need to look again at Jesus as revealed in the Gospels. John helps us see that eternal life is defined as knowing God relationally through Jesus Christ, which means that believing in Jesus is much more than intellectual assent (17:3). True belief includes wholehearted discipleship.

A sheepfold made out of stone

Acts

Spirit-Empowered Witnesses to the World

Central Teaching

Acts tells the story of how God's Spirit worked through the apostles and other early Christians to spread the good news of Christ from Jerusalem to the whole world.

Memory Verse

> *But you will receive power when the Holy Spirit comes on you; and you will be my witnesses in Jerusalem, and in all Judea and Samaria, and to the ends of the earth. (Acts 1:8)*

A Roman road near the ancient city of Gerasa, now the Jordanian city of Jerash

Setting

Luke, the well-educated Gentile, physician, and missionary coworker of the apostle Paul, wrote both Luke and Acts. Both volumes are addressed to "most excellent Theophilus," a recent convert who needed to be instructed and encouraged in his faith (Luke 1:3; Acts 1:1).

Most scholars date the book of Acts between AD 70 and 90. The abrupt ending of the book reflects Luke's literary purpose of showing Paul's arrival in Rome. Traditionally, most evangelicals date the book to around AD 62–64, concluding that Luke finished the book while Paul was still in prison awaiting the outcome of his appeal to Caesar.

Message

Luke's purpose in Acts coincides with his purpose in the Gospel of Luke: to show that God's redemptive work that began in Jesus continues through the Spirit-filled church (Acts 1:1–2). More specifically, Luke provides in Acts a "theological history" of the early church. He tells the story of the early church accurately but selectively for theological purposes (i.e., to show what God is doing). Acts 1:8 reflects the expansion of the gospel, first in Jerusalem and Judea (Acts 1–7), then to surrounding areas (8–12), and finally to the ends of the earth (13–28). Acts is a unique window into the world of the first Christians. The real hero is not Peter or Paul but the Holy Spirit, who works through flawed but committed people to accomplish the mission. The final words of Acts reflect the success of the gospel even while its messengers remain in prison: Paul "proclaimed the kingdom of God and taught about the Lord Jesus Christ—with all boldness and without hindrance!" (Acts 28:31).

Outline

- The coming of the Spirit and his work through the apostles (1:1–4:37)
- Early threats to the church (5:1–6:7)
- God works through Stephen and Philip (6:8–8:40)
- The conversion of Paul (9:1–31)
- The ministry of Peter and the spread of the gospel (9:32–12:25)
- Paul's first missionary journey (13:1–14:28)
- The Jerusalem Council (15:1–35)
- Paul's second missionary journey (15:36–18:22)
- Paul's third missionary journey (18:23–21:16)
- Paul's witness in Jerusalem, Caesarea, and Rome (21:17–28:31)

Interesting Features

- Acts describes the first Christian generation—the period between Jesus's crucifixion (about AD 30) and Paul's first imprisonment in Rome (mid-60s).
- The two main human characters in Acts are Peter (Acts 1–12) and Paul (Acts 13–28). Peter ministers mostly in a Jewish setting while Paul ministers predominantly in a Gentile setting.
- The "speeches" of Peter, Paul, and others make up nearly one-third of the book.

Connections

We obviously don't want to duplicate every early-church pattern we find in Acts (e.g., casting lots or experiencing the judgment of Ananias and Sapphira), but we do want to embrace everything in Acts that should be normative for Christians today. The best way to determine what is normative is to look for those themes in the book that are repeated: the work of the Holy Spirit, the importance of the church, God's sovereignty, persisting in prayer, being a faithful witness, carrying the gospel to all nations, and enduring trials in the cause of Christ. As a result of considering repeated themes in Acts, we learn to follow the Spirit, trust in God's sovereignty, join with God's people, pray, give witness to what God has done in Christ, and be willing to suffer in order to take the message to all people.

"When daylight came, they did not recognize the land, but they saw a bay with a sandy beach, where they decided to run the ship aground if they could" (Acts 27:39). St. Paul's Bay on Malta is a possible location of the shipwreck on Paul's journey to Rome.

Romans

The Good News of God's Righteousness

Central Teaching

God's good news is that in Christ he offers us forgiveness of sins and membership in his new covenant community and promises never to condemn or stop loving us.

Memory Verses

> ***Therefore, there is now no condemnation for those who are in Christ Jesus, because through Christ Jesus the law of the Spirit who gives life has set you free from the law of sin and death. (Rom. 8:1–2)***

Setting

Paul wrote Romans from Corinth around AD 57, with Tertius serving as his scribe (1:1; 16:22). The church in Rome probably originated either from converts on the day of Pentecost who carried the gospel to Rome or from anonymous Christian missionaries. The first Christians in Rome were Jewish Christians, but after Emperor Claudius expelled the Jews from Rome in AD 49, the Gentile Christians had to assume leadership responsibilities in the church. Later, when the Jewish Christians returned, the church struggled with division. Paul writes to this group of house churches with a Gentile Christian majority and Jewish-Christian minority in the hope of unifying them around the gospel of Christ—a unified church would better embody the gospel (15:5–12) and more ably assist him financially for a possible mission trip to Spain (15:22–29).

Message

Paul's Letter to the Romans is probably the clearest and most powerful statement of the gospel in the New Testament. Rather than affirming human potential or innate goodness apart from God, Paul asserts that the gospel begins with bad news: humans are thoroughly sinful, guilty, and without hope. But God came to our rescue in Jesus Christ. He did something for us that we could never do for ourselves. He offers us forgiveness and membership in his covenant community and promises never to condemn us or stop loving us.

Paul hopes this clear and comprehensive explanation of the gospel of Jesus Christ will refocus Jewish and Gentile Christians in Rome on what is most important—the good news of Christ. As a result, a church unified around the gospel of Christ will be a church that

An orchard of pruned olive trees. In Romans 11 Paul compares Israel and the church to an olive tree.

is intentional and passionate about carrying out the Great Commission (i.e., gospel → unity → mission).

This inscription honors Erastus (Rom. 16:23), who was the director of public works in Corinth.

Outline

- Introduction (1:1–17)
- Our problem: all are sinful and guilty (1:18–3:20)
- God's solution: righteousness in Christ (3:21–5:21)
- The result: our participation with Christ (6:1–8:39)
- An important concern: God has been faithful to keep his promises (9:1–11:36)
- Practical implications: relational righteousness (12:1–15:13)
- Conclusion (15:14–16:27)

Interesting Features

- Romans is the longest and most theologically profound of Paul's Letters.
- The letter contains extensive treatments of significant biblical themes: human sinfulness, justification by faith (the doctrine that sparked the Protestant Reformation), life in the Spirit, and God's relationship to Israel.
- Romans emphasizes the gospel or "good news" of God in the beginning of the book (1:1, 2, 9, 15–17), the middle (2:16; 10:15, 16; 11:28), and the end (15:16, 19–20; 16:25).

Connections

Almost every aspect of the Christian life is touched on in this amazing letter. The four Gospels tell the story of Jesus's life, ministry, death, and resurrection, but Romans explains the theological and practical significance of that story. We are reminded of how sinful and hopeless we are apart from God's intervention. We hear again of the amazing graciousness of God to rescue us from our sins and bring us into his covenant family; we can now participate with Jesus in his death and resurrection and experience new life by the power of the Holy Spirit. Moreover, we are challenged to respond to God's grace with a lifestyle of worship and devotion. Throughout history, God has used Romans to change the lives not only of famous believers (e.g., Augustine, Martin Luther, John Wesley, Karl Barth) but also of many much less famous followers. One thing is certain: reading, studying, and meditating upon Romans will change our lives!

Statue of Paul in the Basilica of St. Paul Outside the Walls in Rome

1 Corinthians

Dealing with Church Issues

Central Teaching

A true understanding of what it means to be spiritual will lead to healthy, harmonious relationships within the local church.

Memory Verses

> *Love is patient, love is kind. It does not envy, it does not boast, it is not proud. It does not dishonor others, it is not self-seeking, it is not easily angered, it keeps no record of wrongs. Love does not delight in evil but rejoices with the truth. It always protects, always trusts, always hopes, always perseveres.*
>
> *Love never fails. (1 Cor. 13:4–8)*

Setting

Paul and his coworkers planted the church in Corinth on his second missionary journey (Acts 18:1–18). The city of Corinth was a wealthy melting pot of cultures, philosophies, lifestyles, and religions, and it was especially well known for its sexual immorality (to "Corinthianize" meant to "play the prostitute"). In this pluralistic setting, Paul started what would turn out to be his most challenging church. Paul, along with Sosthenes, is identified as the author (1 Cor. 1:1) and most likely wrote this letter from Ephesus about AD 54 while on his third missionary journey.

Message

Paul had received disturbing verbal reports from Chloe's household (1:11) and a letter from the Corinthians expressing a number of concerns. The church at Corinth was wracked by problems caused by faulty beliefs, arrogance, and immaturity. In response, Paul wrote 1 Corinthians, where he

Ruins of the temple to Apollo in Corinth

wrestles with significant problems in a believing community that is still struggling to separate from its pagan culture. The main problem in both letters (1–2 Corinthians) revolves around the issue of what it means to be truly "spiritual." The Corinthians seem to have embraced a "spirituality" that included intellectual pride and emphasized exciting experiences (see 1 Cor. 8:1, 7, 10–11; 13:2). Some felt they had already "arrived" spiritually, and this overly triumphant attitude explains, for example, why they divided into rival factions (1 Cor. 1:11–12) and why they prided themselves on displaying the more spectacular gifts of the Spirit (1 Cor. 4:8; 13:1). Such an immature understanding of true spirituality led to a variety of problems within the church. In this bold and transparent letter, Paul models how to deal with local church issues in a loving and truthful way.

A bronze statue depicting a Greek "thermae boxer" (third to second century BC)

Outline

- Greeting and thanksgiving (1:1–9)
- Paul responds to reports about the church (1:10–6:20)
- Paul responds to the letter from the Corinthians (7:1–16:4)
- Concluding matters (16:5–24)

Interesting Features

- Overall, Paul wrote more words to the Corinthian church than to any other church.
- In the midst of the most comprehensive discussion of spiritual gifts in the New Testament (1 Cor. 12–14) stands the famous "love chapter" (1 Cor. 13).
- First Corinthians 15 gives more detail on the resurrection of the dead than any other place in the Bible.
- First Corinthians also contains the longest discussion of human sexuality in all of Paul's Letters (1 Cor. 6–7).

Connections

From 1 Corinthians we learn that there is no room for personality cults in the local church; the allegiance to charismatic leaders leads to division and draws praise away from our Lord. We also learn that God expects his people to be holy, which is revealed through the issues Paul addresses in the letter: factions (1–4), incest (5), lawsuits (6:1–11), and sexual immorality (6:12–20). Paul also teaches us that our freedom as believers should be limited by our love for other believers. We are part of a community and not free to act in a way that destroys the faith of family members.

Finally, we need a biblical view of the doctrine of the bodily resurrection of all believers at the return of Christ. Our hope as believers is not death or even rapture but resurrection from the dead!

2 Corinthians

Defending a God-Given Ministry

A bust from Corinth showing one example of hairstyles

Central Teaching

At times, we must defend our God-given ministry for the sake of the gospel and the long-term health of the church.

Memory Verses

But he said to me, "My grace is sufficient for you, for my power is made perfect in weakness." Therefore I will boast all the more gladly about my weaknesses, so that Christ's power may rest on me. That is why, for Christ's sake, I delight in weaknesses, in insults, in hardships, in persecutions, in difficulties. For when I am weak, then I am strong. (2 Cor. 12:9–10)

Setting

Paul, along with Timothy, is identified as the author of 2 Corinthians (1:1). Most contemporary scholars conclude that Paul wrote all of 2 Corinthians, although some see 2 Corinthians 1–9 and 10–13 as separate letters because of the abrupt change in tone. However, good arguments can be made for the unity of 2 Corinthians, especially since it is likely that Paul wrote the letter over a period of time in which he learned of new developments in the church.

After Paul wrote 1 Corinthians, his relationship with the church deteriorated significantly, thanks to some stubborn opponents. Paul probably made a short visit to Corinth from Ephesus (the "painful" visit of 2 Cor. 2:1) and followed up with another letter (the tearful letter of 2 Cor. 2:4; 7:8–9). Most likely, Paul wrote 2 Corinthians from Macedonia around AD 55–56. This means that 2 Corinthians is actually Paul's fourth letter written to this difficult church (a previous letter mentioned in 1 Cor. 5:9, 1 Corinthians, the tearful letter, and 2 Corinthians).

The harbor in Cenchrea

Message

At the time when Paul wrote 2 Corinthians, some of the Corinthians who had previously questioned Paul's apostleship appear to have repented and now support Paul (2 Cor. 2:5, 8–9; 5:12; 7:2–16). Nevertheless, a minority within the church still question whether Paul is a legitimate apostle (perhaps addressed in 2 Cor. 10–13). In addition, a number of false apostles have arrived in Corinth, and they must be countered (11:1–15). In a deeply personal and

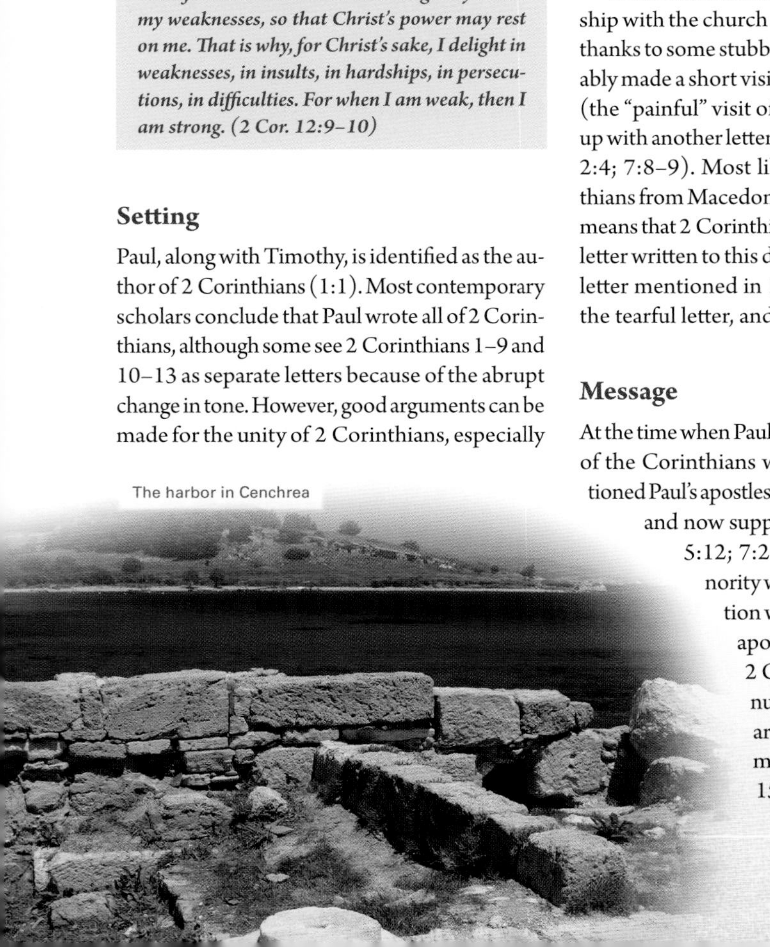

The bema (or judgment seat) in Corinth, where Paul appeared before the proconsul Gallio (Acts 18:12–17)

emotional letter, Paul defends his authority as a genuine apostle of Jesus Christ as well as his way of life and ministry—a measure he is forced to take because the gospel and the spiritual life of the Corinthians are at stake.

Second Corinthians speaks volumes about the heart of Christian ministry and the value of seeking reconciliation. Paul suffered greatly in the cause of Christ, and he cares deeply about the Corinthians. He's not willing to give up on them. He speaks the truth in love while keeping his heart open to the possibility of reconciliation.

Outline

- Greeting and thanksgiving (1:1–11)
- Paul's apostolic conduct and ministry (1:12–7:16)
- The Corinthians' generous giving (8:1–9:15)
- Paul's apostolic authority (10:1–13:10)
- Conclusion (13:11–14)

Interesting Features

- Second Corinthians is probably the most personal of all of Paul's Letters.
- Second Corinthians 8–9 is one of the primary New Testament passages related to financial giving.
- This letter reminds us that reconciliation can be personally painful, disruptive to ministry plans, and dependent on other people's responses, but it's worth pursuing.

Connections

In 2 Corinthians we are reminded that sometimes ministry doesn't line up with our expectations. People cast doubt on our motives, misconstrue our actions, and turn other believers against us. Paul models how to struggle through this ministerial mess. He embraces weakness and suffering as legitimate badges of authentic ministry, but he is also willing to defend himself when important things—such as the gospel and the spiritual well-being of believers—are at stake. While there are times when conflict is unavoidable and even essential to long-term healthy relationships within the body of Christ, reconciliation is our goal. However, our focus should be on the integrity of our beliefs and our actions.

Galatians

Liberated to Love

Central Teaching

We have been set free by the work of Christ to walk by the Spirit, who will empower us to love, which is the deepest demonstration of true spirituality.

Memory Verse

> ***You, my brothers and sisters, were called to be free. But do not use your freedom to indulge the flesh; rather, serve one another humbly in love. (Gal. 5:13)***

Setting

Paul writes to the "churches of Galatia" (1:1–2; 5:2), which are likely the same churches he started on his first missionary journey (Acts 13–14). When did Paul write Galatians? The answer depends on how Paul's visits to Jerusalem that are mentioned in Galatians are matched with those mentioned in Acts. The following statements outline two main possibilities:

- Galatians 2 corresponds with Acts 11 (early date)—Paul wrote Galatians from Syrian Antioch soon after his first missionary journey in about AD 48–49. The first two visits in Galatians match the first two visits in Acts, and Galatians was written prior to the Jerusalem Council (Acts 15).
- Galatians 2 corresponds with Acts 15 (late date)—Paul wrote Galatians during his third missionary journey, between AD 53 and 58. The second Jerusalem visit mentioned in Galatians matches the third visit recorded in Acts and puts Galatians after the Jerusalem Council.

We subscribe to the early date, making Galatians the earliest of Paul's Letters.

Message

The crisis in the Galatian churches involves three key players: the apostle Paul, the false teachers, and the Galatian Christians. When Paul first preached the gospel of Christ crucified to the Galatians, they accepted him, believed the gospel, and received the Holy Spirit—a sign of God's blessing. But soon after, false teachers arrived and demanded that these new Gentile Christians submit to circumcision (5:2–4; 6:12–13) and other religious requirements (4:9–10)

The theater at Pisidian Antioch, a city in the Roman province of Galatia

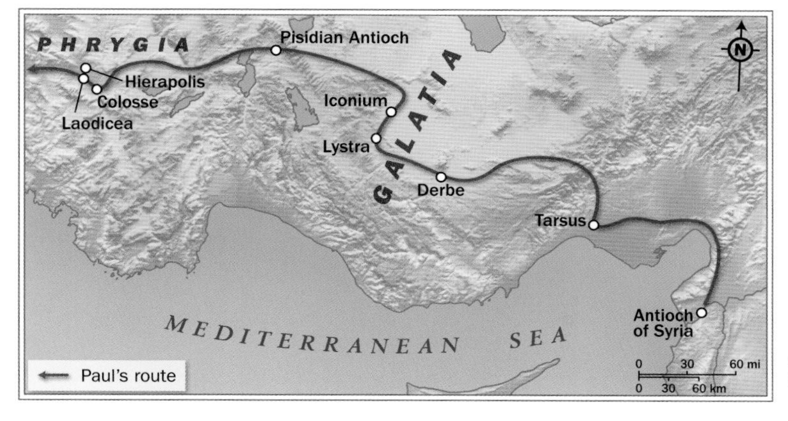

Paul's travels to Galatia

for full Christian status. Their childlike faith in Christ was in the process of being replaced by attempts to keep the law (3:3).

In response, Paul defends his apostleship and authority (1:1–2:14) because the integrity of the gospel is connected to the integrity of the preacher. Next, he clarifies the true gospel (2:15–4:11), arguing that real righteousness—and the freedom it brings—comes only through faith in Christ, the faithful one. Paul then calls the Galatians to decide (4:11–6:10), urging them to walk by the Spirit who can empower them to love, the true indicator of authentic spirituality.

Outline

- Letter opening and occasion for the letter (1:1–10)
- Divine origin of Paul's apostleship and gospel (1:11–2:14)
- Righteousness by faith and supporting arguments (2:15–4:11)
- Personal appeal: "Become like me" (4:12–20)
- Scriptural appeal: children of the free woman (4:21–31)
- Ethical appeal (5:1–6:10)
- Letter closing: compromise or the cross (6:11–18)

Interesting Features

- Galatians may be Paul's earliest letter.
- The letter reminds us that the integrity of the gospel and the integrity of Christian leaders are closely connected.
- The "works of the flesh" and "fruit of the Spirit" lists are found in Galatians (5:19–23).
- Paul discusses the relationship between law and grace in this letter.
- Galatians emphasizes that Spirit-empowered love fulfills the law.

Connections

Galatians reminds us that the one true gospel centers upon the atoning death of Jesus Christ. Christ has set us free, and nothing we do can be added to the work of Christ. We become children of God not by performing works of religious law but by trusting Christ personally. In Galatians, we are reminded that we continue the Christian life the same way we began the Christian life—by depending upon God's grace to transform us. It's not that Jesus saves us, and then we have to perfect ourselves by moral effort. From beginning to end, we depend on the Lord in faith. We're now free to follow the Spirit, who will transform and empower us to love people. Love fulfills the law, God's holy standard.

Ephesians

New Life and New Community in Christ

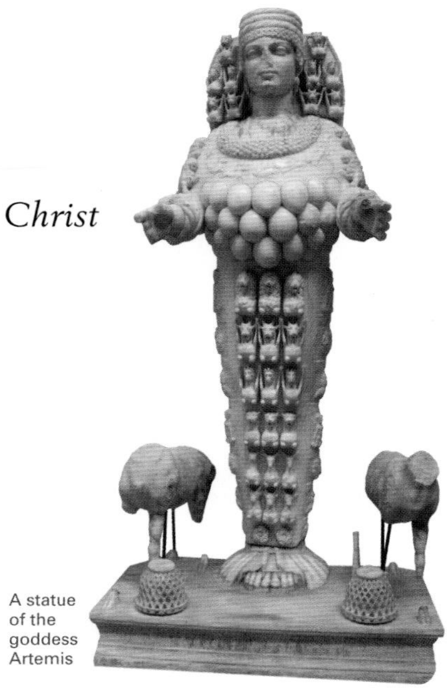
A statue of the goddess Artemis

Central Teaching

God's magnificent plan to offer new life and new community is achieved through Christ and demonstrated in the life of the church.

Memory Verses

> ***For it is by grace you have been saved, through faith—and this is not from yourselves, it is the gift of God—not by works, so that no one can boast. For we are God's handiwork, created in Christ Jesus to do good works, which God prepared in advance for us to do. (Eph. 2:8–10)***

Setting

Paul claims to be the author of Ephesians (1:1–2; 3:1), and its authenticity as one of his genuine letters was well attested by the early church. Paul was a prisoner when he penned Ephesians (see 3:1; 4:1; 6:20), and the traditional view that he wrote the letter (along with the other prison letters) from Rome around AD 60–62 while under house arrest remains the most likely scenario. Paul probably intended Ephesians to circulate among various churches in Asia Minor as a masterful summary of the faith and an encouragement to believers.

Message

Paul didn't write Ephesians to solve a major problem or to deal with any particular emergency but to encourage believers to understand and experience three important spiritual realities:

1. *The new life we have in Christ.* Through the life, death, and resurrection of Christ, God fulfills his plan to rescue people from sin and Satan. The Holy Spirit makes this plan a personal reality for those who respond to God's gracious offer by faith in Christ.
2. *The new community we are connected to in Christ.* God has not only given new life to individuals in Christ, but he has also created a new community, comprised of both Jews and Gentiles. Paul stresses the new community through words like "unity," "one," "with," and "together with," as well as through concepts such as church, body, temple, and bride. When we are reconciled to Christ, we become part of God's new covenant community.
3. *The new walk our community is called to by Christ.* God's magnificent plan to give new life and create a new community in Christ (Eph. 1–3) results in a new way of life for the believer (Eph. 4–6). This new community is maintained and preserved as we live or walk in unity, holiness, light, wisdom, and the Lord's strength.

Curetes street in Ancient Ephesus

Outline

- Letter opening (1:1–2)
- Praise for spiritual blessings in Christ (1:3–14)
- Prayer for spiritual understanding (1:15–23)
- New life in Christ (2:1–10)
- New community in Christ (2:11–22)
- Paul's unique role in God's plan (3:1–13)
- Paul's prayer for the new community (3:14–21)
- New walk in Christ (4:1–6:20)
- Letter closing (6:21–24)

Interesting Features

- Paul stresses our identity in Christ and our unity in Christ with expressions such as "in Christ," "in him," and "in whom" (these phrases occur nearly forty times).
- Paul emphasizes the universal nature of the church (see 1:22; 3:10, 21; 5:23–25, 27, 29, 32, as well as images like body, building, temple, and new humanity).
- Ephesians shares many common themes with Colossians (e.g., compare Col. 3:18–4:1 with Eph. 5:22–6:9).
- Ephesians tells us how the Christian faith should be lived out in the household (5:21–6:9).

Relief featuring a soldier's armor

Connections

This rich letter reminds us that we are transformed by God's grace and that we accept this life-changing gift by faith. So many religions in our world are based on human effort and performance—that is, what we can do for God. But Ephesians boldly reminds us that we are changed by what God has done for us in Christ. God not only rescues us from sin, but he also brings us into a new community. In this new community and in light of all that God has done for us, we are called to live a life worthy of what we have received in Christ, all to the glory and praise of God.

Philippians

A Joyful Thank-You Letter

Central Teaching

In this personal letter, Paul thanks the Philippians for their generous support, gives them a personal update, and exhorts them to greater unity and joy in Christ.

Memory Verses

> *Do nothing out of selfish ambition or vain conceit. Rather, in humility value others above yourselves, not looking to your own interests but each of you to the interests of the others.*
>
> *In your relationships with one another, have the same mindset as Christ Jesus. (Phil. 2:3–5)*

Setting

The apostle Paul likely wrote Philippians during his first Roman imprisonment around AD 60–62, perhaps near the end of his time in chains. He founded the church at Philippi on his second missionary journey (see Acts 16:12–40), and this church supported him financially more than any other (2 Cor. 8:1–5; 11:8–9; Phil. 4:10–19), staying loyal to Paul through the most difficult times of his ministry (Acts 16:19–24, 35–40; Phil. 1:29–30). While visiting Paul, Epaphroditus (a visitor from Philippi) became gravely ill and almost died (2:26–27, 30). After he recovered, Paul sent him back to the Philippians (2:26, 28–30), using this opportunity to say "thank you" to the Philippians through this pastoral letter.

Message

Many believers name Philippians as their favorite letter from Paul, for this personal correspondence to a group of close friends touches our hearts in many ways. Paul reminds his friends that although he is in prison, the gospel is not; God continues to work mightily in spite of Paul's difficult situation. He thanks them for their generous support and exhorts them to live a life worthy of the gospel. In addition, he stresses the importance of unity by highlighting the humility of Christ, which produces unity within the church. Paul warns the Philippians against trusting in their own righteousness and directs them to rely on Christ's righteousness on their behalf, challenging them to follow his example of forgetting the past and pressing on toward Christlikeness as they anticipate Christ's return. Along the way, Paul offers practical insight on Christian living, such as choosing to rejoice rather than worry and making peace instead of grumbling.

A relief of Nike, the goddess of victory

Outline

- ▸ Letter opening, thanksgiving, and prayer (1:1–11)
- ▸ Paul's circumstances and attitude (1:12–26)
- ▸ Living in a manner worthy of the gospel (1:27–30)
- ▸ Appeal to imitate Christ's humility, which leads to unity (2:1–30)
- ▸ Warning against false teachers (3:1–6)
- ▸ Righteousness from God (3:7–11)
- ▸ Press on toward the goal (3:12–4:1)
- ▸ Concluding exhortations and letter closing (4:2–23)

The Via Egnatia, which passed through Philippi

Interesting Features

- In one of the most eloquent and powerful passages in the entire New Testament, Philippians 2:5–11 describes the humiliation and exaltation of Jesus Christ.
- Paul draws on Philippi's special privileges as a Roman colony to emphasize the importance of our heavenly citizenship (1:27; 3:20).
- The theme of joy appears throughout the letter ("joy" in 1:4, 25; 2:2, 29; 4:1; "rejoice" or "rejoice with" in 1:18; 2:17–18, 28; 3:1; 4:4, 10).
- Philippians stresses the return of the Lord (1:6, 10; 2:9–11, 16; 3:20–21; 4:5).

Connections

There are numerous ways that Philippians applies to us. We can partner in the work of the gospel by supporting missionaries financially as the Philippians supported Paul. From the apostle's example, we can learn to stay faithful in difficult circumstances and to rejoice that God is bringing good out of a tough situation. Philippians also reminds us of the importance of unity within the body of Christ—a unity that is made possible through our imitation of Christ's humility and our service to one another (2:1–11). Lastly, the letter reminds us that we haven't arrived in the Christian life. No matter what our past, we should neither be enslaved by it nor be overly confident in it. We're still on a journey. Rather, we should obey God in our present circumstances, knowing that he is always working within and among us and that he has a wonderful future in store.

Colossians

The Supremacy and Sufficiency of Christ

Central Teaching

Jesus Christ is the supreme revelation of God, and he is sufficient for the deepest experience of life with God.

Memory Verses

> ***For in Christ all the fullness of the Deity lives in bodily form, and in Christ you have been brought to fullness. He is the head over every power and authority. (Col. 2:9–10)***

Setting

Colossians was probably written by Paul during his first Roman imprisonment, around AD 60–62. Since Tychicus carried both Ephesians and Colossians (and likely Philemon) to their respective readers, all three letters must have been written from the same place (Eph. 6:21–22; Col. 4:7–9). Epaphras probably planted the church in Colossae (Col. 1:7; 4:12–13) and later visited Paul in Rome with a report on the Colossian church (Philem. 23). Although Epaphras had many positive things to report (Col. 1:8; 2:5), he also raised serious concerns about a false teaching that was threatening the church. Paul wrote Colossians to counter this heresy and to exalt Christ as head of the church.

Message

According to Paul, the dangerous teaching threatening the church at Colossae gives Christ "a place" but not "the place." Paul never explicitly defines this heresy, but his response in the letter leads us to conclude that it emphasizes

The theater at Hierapolis, a city in Asia Minor only a short distance from Colossae (Col. 4:13)

"fine-sounding arguments" (2:4, 8), private visions and special knowledge (2:18, 23), mystical experience (2:8, 18), and strict rules and regulations—even ascetic practices (2:16–17, 21–23). Paul labels the false teaching a "hollow and deceptive philosophy, which depends on human tradition and the elemental spiritual forces of this world rather than on Christ" (2:8).

Paul emphasizes that Christ is supreme over all other spiritual powers and is sufficient for the Colossian Christians. A false knowledge of Christ must be countered by a full knowledge of Christ. The many qualities of Christ (described in 1:15–22; 2:3, 8–10, 15, 17; and 3:1) stand in contrast to particular aspects of the false philosophy.

Outline

- Letter opening (1:1–2)
- Thanksgiving and prayer (1:3–14)
- The supremacy of Christ (1:15–23)
- Paul's mission and concern for the Colossians (1:24–2:5)
- The solution to false teaching: fullness in Christ (2:6–23)
- The Christian's new life in Christ (3:1–17)
- The Christian household (3:18–4:1)
- Further instructions (4:2–6)
- Letter closing (4:7–18)

Bust of the ancient Greek philosopher Epicurus

Interesting Features

- Paul writes to a church he never visited (Col. 2:1).
- Because the supremacy of Christ is the main theme of Colossians, it includes more about the person of Jesus Christ than most of Paul's Letters.
- Colossians has much in common with Ephesians (e.g., Col. 3:18–4:1 and Eph. 5:22–6:9). While Colossians emphasizes Christ as the head of the church, Ephesians focuses on the church as the body of Christ.
- Paul includes a section on how Christians should live within their own households (3:18–4:1).

Connections

The message of Colossians applies extremely well to believers and churches threatened by false teaching, a very common occurrence in our day. Because some Christians are heavily influenced by folk religion or pagan ideas (e.g., magic or astrology), they live in fear when their horoscopes predict bad events. They are more concerned with fate, fortune cookies, luck, and superstition than they are with the words of Christ. Perhaps even more believers are in bondage to religious rules and regulations, though human commands have no power to encourage true spirituality. We live in a syncretistic age in which various ideas blend together to provide false teachers with plenty of material for their deceptions. Colossians states truly and boldly that Christ is supreme over all so-called gods and powers; he is sufficient for every believer! Christians have been given spiritual fullness in Christ, so there is no need to search for a spiritual supplement.

1 Thessalonians

Living in Light of Christ's Second Coming: Part One

Central Teaching

Because of the hope we have in Christ—hope that will be fulfilled at his return—we should seek to please the Lord by loving one another and persevering in faith.

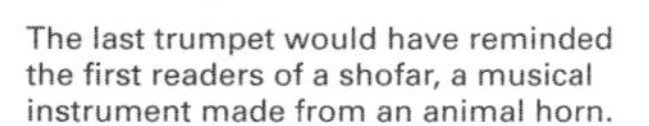

The last trumpet would have reminded the first readers of a shofar, a musical instrument made from an animal horn.

Memory Verses

> ***For the Lord himself will come down from heaven . . . and the dead in Christ will rise first. After that, we who are still alive and are left will be caught up together with them in the clouds to meet the Lord in the air. And so we will be with the Lord forever. Therefore encourage one another with these words. (1 Thess. 4:16–18)***

Setting

Both 1 and 2 Thessalonians come from "Paul, Silas and Timothy" (1 Thess. 1:1; 2 Thess. 1:1), but the content of the letters and the use of "I" throughout indicate that Paul is probably the lead author. Shortly after founding the church in Thessalonica (see Acts 17:1–10), Paul and Silas left because of violent opposition from the Jews. The young, fragile church faced strong external pressure, and Paul feared for their spiritual safety. On numerous occasions he tried (unsuccessfully) to return to Thessalonica, but he resorted to sending Timothy instead. In time, Timothy returned to Paul with good news—the believers in Thessalonica were staying strong, but they needed encouragement and additional instruction. Paul writes both letters from Corinth in the early AD 50s with the purpose of encouraging and instructing these new believers.

Message

Both 1 and 2 Thessalonians are devoted to encouragement and instruction concerning how to live in light of the return (or *parousia*) of the Lord Jesus. In Paul we see the heart of a pastor for a local congregation that is facing external persecution and wrestling with internal issues. After defending the truth of the gospel and the integrity of his apostleship, Paul expresses genuine concern for the Thessalonians and urges them to please the Lord as they live in light of his second coming. In chapters 4–5, Paul reminds them that although believers grieve at the death of fellow believers, they grieve in hope because of Christ's resurrection. He then instructs them concerning what is to come. First, Christ will *return*, and then he will *resurrect* his people who have died and transform those still alive at his coming. Christ's return will be public, visible, and unmistakable. It will be followed by the *rapture* (or gathering) of Christ's people to himself and an eternal *reunion* with the Lord. Believers should be alert and self-controlled so as not to be surprised by Jesus's coming. God has not appointed his children to suffer wrath but to experience salvation and eternal life.

Outline

- Letter opening and thanksgiving (1:1–10)
- Paul's faithful ministry among the Thessalonians (2:1–16)
- Paul's ongoing concern for the Thessalonians (2:17–3:13)
- Instructions about pleasing the Lord (4:1–12)
- Questions about Christ's return (4:13–5:11)
- Final instructions about church life (5:12–22)
- Letter closing (5:23–28)

Interesting Features

- This may have been Paul's earliest letter (AD 51), depending on when Galatians is dated.
- Paul mentions the theme of the second coming of Christ at the end of each chapter (1:10; 2:19; 3:13; 4:13–18; 5:23).
- Both 1 and 2 Thessalonians are addressed to new believers who are facing trials, and both letters urge them to endure in hope.

Connections

While some Christians are consumed with matters related to the end times, others seem to have forgotten that Jesus is coming back. We grieve the brokenness of this world, but one day Christ will return to conquer death once and for all; he will make all things new. Our priorities should not involve trying to predict the exact time of Christ's return but striving to live faithfully, doing what God has told us to do.

Paul asks, "What is . . . the crown in which we will glory?" (1 Thess. 2:19). In Rome, to receive an oak leaf wreath or crown was a high honor given to those who had saved the life of a Roman solider in battle by an unusual act of courage. This gold oak wreath was found in Turkey (350–300 BC).

2 Thessalonians

Living in Light of Christ's Second Coming: Part Two

Central Teaching

Paul passes along true and reliable teachings related to Christ's return and encourages Christians to persevere in responsible and righteous living as they anticipate his return.

Memory Verses

> ***But the Lord is faithful, and he will strengthen you and protect you from the evil one. We have confidence in the Lord that you are doing and will continue to do the things we command. May the Lord direct your hearts into God's love and Christ's perseverance.*** *(2 Thess. 3:3–5)*

Bust of the Roman emperor Caligula, who reigned from AD 37 to 41. Paul says in 2 Thessalonians 2:4 that the man of lawlessness "sets himself up in God's temple, proclaiming himself to be God," similar to what Caligula attempted to do in the Jerusalem temple.

Setting

Between the writing of 1 and 2 Thessalonians, it appears that external pressure had grown stronger (1:3–10) and some of Paul's teachings had been misunderstood, particularly those concerning Christ's return. Someone was confusing the Thessalonians by teaching that the "day of the Lord" had actually arrived (2:1–2). This must have been an attractive thought for people wanting to be delivered from persecution and may explain why some of them were disrupting the community (3:6–15). Paul wrote 2 Thessalonians to correct the false teaching about the Lord's return and to help believers get their priorities straight as they anticipated his coming. Like 1 Thessalonians, this second letter was likely written from Corinth in the early AD 50s.

Message

Paul taught the Thessalonians about Christ's second coming in his first letter, but they became confused and worried (likely through the influence of false teachers) that the day of the Lord had already arrived. Was the persecution they were suffering part of God's judgment against them? Paul reassures them that Christ will not return until certain events take place: "the rebellion" (2:3) must occur, and the "man of lawlessness" (2:3) must first be revealed. The "rebellion" refers to a falling away from God, and "the man of lawlessness" generally corresponds to other New Testament accounts of an end-time enemy of God (the antichrist in 1 John 2:18 and the "beast . . . of the sea" in Rev. 13:1). For the time being, this figure is restrained in some way (2 Thess. 2:7).

Paul also instructs the church to keep away from those who are engaged in selfish and divisive behavior and to follow his example of working hard in a way that will benefit the community.

Paul reassures the believers that God has chosen and called them to experience salvation through the work of the Spirit and belief in the truth, and he challenges them to stand firm and hold fast to the teachings they previously received.

Outline

- Letter opening, thanksgiving, and prayer (1:1–12)
- Instructions about events leading up to Christ's return (2:1–12)
- Reassurance and prayer for believers (2:13–3:5)
- Warning against disruptive behavior (3:6–15)
- Letter closing (3:16–18)

Interesting Features

- Paul mentions several "hot topics" related to the second coming of Jesus, such as the day of the Lord, the rebellion, the man of lawlessness, and the restraining person or influence (2:7).
- Misconceptions about the return of Christ can lead to disruptive and unfaithful living on the part of some. About 40 percent of this letter deals with Christ's return.
- In this quick follow-up to 1 Thessalonians, Paul reminds us of the importance of explaining our theology clearly and persistently.

Connections

Even the best pastors are at times misunderstood, and even the best pastors must occasionally use tough love. In this letter Paul speaks truthfully and plainly and boldly to bring wisdom and balance to the issue of Christ's second coming. He reminds us that while we should live in the light of the hope of Christ's return, this should not cause us to live selfishly. We should continue to live wisely and faithfully as we anticipate his coming. Biblical eschatology always leads to biblical ethics rather than to self-centered escapism.

Remains from the marketplace in Thessalonica

1 Timothy

Teach the Truth

Central Teaching

Paul writes to stop the false teaching in the church and to teach the church how to conduct itself.

Memory Verses

But you, man of God, flee from all this, and pursue righteousness, godliness, faith, love, endurance and gentleness. Fight the good fight of the faith. Take hold of the eternal life to which you were called when you made your good confession in the presence of many witnesses. (1 Tim. 6:11–12)

Setting

First and Second Timothy and Titus are known as the Pastoral Letters because each letter addresses a pastor. Timothy accompanied Paul on his second and third missionary journeys and is listed as cosender in five of Paul's Letters; Timothy was serving as pastor of the church in Ephesus at the time. Titus, a Gentile believer and one of Paul's closest companions in ministry, was serving as pastor on the island of Crete. To these two trusted and dearly loved partners in ministry, Paul wrote three very significant letters dealing with life in the local church.

Sometime between AD 63 and 67, Paul wrote letters to Timothy (in Ephesus) and Titus (in Crete), instructing them about local church ministry and encouraging them to persevere. After Paul was imprisoned a second time, he wrote Timothy one final letter, a farewell to his faithful friend. (See also the "Setting" of 2 Timothy and Titus.)

A bust of Emperor Nero, who was the Roman emperor when Paul wrote the Pastoral Letters

Message

Paul had earlier warned the Ephesian elders that false teachers from their own group would distort the truth and lead people astray (Acts 20:30). According to 1 Timothy 1:3–7, that is exactly what happened. In Ephesus false teaching had become a problem, and the elders were responsible for teaching (1 Tim. 3:1–7; 5:17–25). In other words, the church in Ephesus was being threatened by some of its own leaders.

After challenging Timothy to teach the truth (1:3–20), Paul gives instructions about worship and leadership in the local church (1 Tim. 2–3). He focuses on the theme of godliness (1 Tim. 4), which is perhaps the most significant quality for any effective church leader. In the closing chapters Paul is very practical and offers corrective instructions for several groups, including the elders of the church. Throughout, Paul challenges Timothy to be the leader God wants him to be by not showing favoritism, keeping himself pure, teaching the truth, resisting temptation, and fighting the good fight of faith.

Outline

- Letter opening (1:1–2)
- Charge to Timothy: teach the truth (1:3–20)
- Instructions about church worship and leadership (2:1–3:16)
- Pursue godliness and avoid false teachings (4:1–16)
- Instructions for groups within the church (5:1–6:2)
- Concluding warnings (6:3–21)

A Roman coin with Nero's portrait

Interesting Features

- Paul presents qualifications and instructions for church leaders (elders and deacons) in 1 Timothy 3:1–13; 5:17–25; and Titus 1:6–9.
- First Timothy 2:11–15 offers a significant (and much debated) passage on the role of women in the church.
- First Timothy 6 contains wise advice about how Christians should use money.
- The Pastorals contain five "trustworthy sayings" (1 Tim. 1:15; 3:1; 4:9; 2 Tim. 2:11; Titus 3:8).

Connections

The Pastoral Letters continue to speak in meaningful ways about life and ministry in the local church, particularly in terms of the various qualifications and responsibilities of church leaders (1 Tim. 3:1–13; Titus 1:5–9). Today, we should pay attention to all the items on these lists rather than being selective about which ones to apply. Along with setting a godly example, certain leaders are charged with teaching the Scriptures faithfully and accurately. Since false teaching continues to threaten the church, thereby steering people away from Christ, it is the leader's job to lovingly shepherd the flock away from danger and back toward God's truth.

2 Timothy

A Final Word to a Faithful Friend

A papyrus scroll. In 2 Timothy 4:13, Paul instructs Timothy to bring his "scrolls, especially the parchments."

Central Teaching

In his final letter, Paul challenges his son in the faith, Timothy, to fight the good fight and finish the course.

Memory Verse

> *All Scripture is God-breathed and is useful for teaching, rebuking, correcting and training in righteousness. (2 Tim. 3:16)*

Setting

All three Pastoral Letters claim Paul as their author, but his authorship has been questioned by many contemporary scholars because the literary style and doctrinal emphases of the letters vary from Paul's other letters. What's more, there is no place in the book of Acts where the Pastorals seem to fit. Nevertheless, solid arguments remain in favor of Pauline authorship of the Pastorals. The letters were likely written after the story told in Acts concludes, and the different subject matter, purposes, and circumstances account for many of the differences. It's also possible that Luke served as Paul's trusted secretary and was given added freedom to compose the letters (2 Tim. 4:11). Paul probably wrote 2 Timothy around AD 67–68 after being imprisoned in Rome a second time and shortly before he was martyred. (See also the "Setting" of 1 Timothy and Titus.)

Message

Whereas Paul's first Roman imprisonment was a house arrest, his second imprisonment seems more severe. Housed in a cold, damp, hard-to-find place, he has been deserted by some and opposed by others. There is a sense that death is at hand, making 2 Timothy a kind of last will and testament. Paul reminds Timothy of the sincere faith passed on to him by his grandmother and mother. He exhorts

The Mamertine Prison in Rome, where Paul may have been imprisoned when he wrote 2 Timothy

Timothy to stay faithful, to work hard in ministry, and to be willing to suffer for the sake of the gospel. He tells Timothy to hold to the sound teachings of the faith, to handle Scripture correctly, and to stay true to the Christ-centered gospel. In addition, Paul warns Timothy of false teachers and charlatans and calls him to pursue godliness as Timothy imitates Paul's teachings and way of life. Paul's last words to Timothy (4:1–18) are packed with emotion as Paul reminds him of his God-given calling, assures him that God is faithful even at the end of a person's life, and pleads with Timothy to come visit him before it's too late. Paul reveals his deep love for his faithful friend and closes his last letter with the expression that characterizes his life perhaps more than any other: "Grace be with you" (4:22).

Outline

- Letter opening (1:1–2)
- Encouragement to stay faithful (1:3–18)
- Be strong in God's grace and endure hardship (2:1–13)
- A workman who correctly handles the Word (2:14–26)
- Persevering in difficult times (3:1–17)
- Paul's final words to Timothy (4:1–18)
- Letter closing (4:19–22)

Interesting Features

- Second Timothy is most likely Paul's final letter, written a short time before he was martyred (see 2 Tim. 4:16–18).
- Second Timothy 3:16–17 offers an extremely important affirmation of the inspiration of Scripture.
- The letter is filled with metaphors for living the Christian life to the very end (e.g., an athletic contest or a battle).

Connections

Paul's final letter calls us to enduring faithfulness in spite of the difficult circumstances of life and ministry. While there will always be false teachers, troublemakers, loved ones near death, and doubts about our own abilities, God remains faithful. In the face of these troubles, Paul points Timothy beyond himself to God's all-sufficient grace to carry on. We, like Timothy, need to fulfill our calling faithfully. We also need to love those under our care, stay true to God's Word, endure opposition, and finish the race marked out for us so that we can say with Paul, "I have fought the good fight, I have finished the race, I have kept the faith" (2 Tim. 4:7).

The starting line used for the Pythian games at Delphi, Greece

Titus

Devote Yourself to Doing Good

Central Teaching

As a powerful witness in a pagan society, Christians should devote themselves to doing what is good.

Memory Verses

For the grace of God has appeared that offers salvation to all people. It teaches us to say "No" to ungodliness and worldly passions, and to live self-controlled, upright and godly lives in this present age, while we wait for the blessed hope—the appearing of the glory of our great God and Savior, Jesus Christ, who gave himself for us to redeem us from all wickedness and to purify for himself a people that are his very own, eager to do what is good. (Titus 2:11–14)

Setting

First and Second Timothy and Titus are known as the Pastoral Letters because each letter addresses a pastor. Titus, a Gentile believer and one of Paul's closest companions in ministry, was serving as pastor on the island of Crete when he received this letter from the apostle.

When the book of Acts closes, Paul is still under house arrest in Rome, awaiting his trial before Caesar (Acts 28:30–31). We are not told how things turned out for Paul, but early church tradition says that Paul was released from prison, continued his ministry for a time, was imprisoned again in Rome, and was eventually martyred (see Eusebius, *Ecclesiastical History*, 2.22.2, 5). The following reconstruction of the historical setting is one way of making sense of the scriptural evidence:

- First Roman imprisonment around AD 60–62 (Acts 28)
- Release from first Roman imprisonment (not recorded in Acts)
- Traveled west (perhaps made it to Spain; see Rom. 15:24, 28)
- Traveled to Crete, left Titus (Titus 1:5)
- Traveled to Miletus (2 Tim. 4:20)
- Traveled to Ephesus, left Timothy (1 Tim. 1:3)
- Traveled to Macedonia (1 Tim. 1:3; Phil. 2:24) and Nicopolis (Titus 3:12)
- Arrested on the way to Ephesus (possibly at Troas; see 2 Tim. 4:13)
- Imprisoned a second time in Rome and martyred during persecution by Nero around AD 67–68 (2 Tim. 1:16–17; 2:9; 4:6–8, 13, 20–21)

The harbor at Fair Havens on the island of Crete

Location of Crete

Sometime between AD 63 and 67, Paul wrote letters to Timothy (in Ephesus) and Titus (in Crete), instructing them about local church ministry and encouraging them to persevere. (See also the "Setting" of 1 and 2 Timothy.)

Message

Paul left Titus on Crete to appoint leaders in the various house churches (1:5). The people of Crete had a reputation for dishonesty, gluttony, and laziness (1:12), so it's no surprise that Paul's focus in the letter to Titus is on how God's people should live in the midst of a pagan society. Christians should devote themselves to doing what is good, which is the main theme of this letter (Titus 1:8, 16; 2:7, 14; 3:1–8, 14). In addition, Paul instructs Titus on matters related to combating false teaching, teaching doctrine, and relationships within the church.

Outline

- ▸ Letter opening (1:1–4)
- ▸ Instructions for groups within the church (1:5–2:15)
- ▸ Devote yourselves to doing good (3:1–11)
- ▸ Letter closing (3:12–15)

Interesting Features

- Paul's letter to Titus repeatedly stresses good works as the normal expression of a genuine Christian faith (see Titus 2:7, 14; 3:1, 8, 14).
- Paul clarifies that the "blessed hope" of all believers is the return of Jesus Christ (2:13).
- Along with 1 Timothy 3:1–13 and 5:17–25, Paul presents qualifications and instructions for church leaders in Titus 1:6–9.

Connections

The Pastoral Letters speak in meaningful ways about life and ministry in the local church. In Titus especially, Paul highlights the importance of doing what is good. We are saved by grace and not by good works, but true believers will devote themselves to doing good works as a demonstration of the genuineness of their faith. Like Paul says in Ephesians, we are saved by grace through faith for good works (Eph. 2:8–10).

Philemon

Equality in Christ

Central Teaching

One's relationship to Christ changes all other relationships, bringing equality among those who are in Christ.

Memory Verses

> ***Perhaps the reason he was separated from you for a little while was that you might have him back forever—no longer as a slave, but better than a slave, as a dear brother. (Philem. 15–16)***

Setting

Paul wrote Philemon most likely when he was a prisoner in Rome in the early AD 60s, about the same time he wrote Ephesians, Colossians, and Philippians. Besides Paul, two main characters appear in this drama. Philemon is the slave owner who became a believer in Colossae through the ministry of Paul (v. 19). Onesimus is the runaway slave who may have stolen from his master (v. 18), come in contact with Paul in Rome, and subsequently become a Christian (v. 10). Paul wrote to persuade Philemon to act in a certain way toward his human slave because they are both brothers in Christ.

Message

What do a Jewish-Christian apostle, a wealthy Gentile slave owner, and a runaway slave have in common? Nothing, unless they are united as brothers in Christ. This short letter tells the story of how one's relationship to Christ changes all other relationships, especially those within the body of Christ.

Paul writes as a "prisoner of Christ" (vv. 1, 9) to persuade Philemon to receive Onesimus as he would receive Paul himself (v. 17), without punishing him or putting him to death, which is typical treatment for runaway slaves under Roman law. Paul wants Philemon to welcome Onesimus as a "dear brother" (v. 16) and perhaps even to set him free to serve in the cause of Christ (v. 21). The phrase "even more" in verse 21 likely hints that Paul wants Philemon to free Onesimus and send him back to assist Paul in mission service.

Rather than calling for the abolition of the institution of Roman slavery, a strategy that may have destroyed the early church, Paul recognizes the evils of human slavery and preaches a gospel that ultimately leads to its downfall. Paul employs clever but powerful rhetorical strategies to persuade Philemon to act redemptively toward his slave. For example, he writes as an "old man" and a "prisoner" in soliciting sympathy in his

The cast of a corpse of a slave (as indicated by the shackles on his ankles) recovered from the ruins of Pompeii

The interior of the Colosseum in Rome, showing what lies beneath the stadium floor

appeal for his "son Onesimus" (vv. 9–10). Just as Philemon has refreshed the hearts of others (v. 7), Paul sends his "very heart" (Onesimus) back to him (v. 12), hoping Philemon will also refresh Paul's heart (v. 20). Paul is equating Philemon and Onesimus as brothers in Christ, thereby putting a slave owner and a slave on the same level. He offers Philemon eternal perspective in the hope that Philemon will honor his requests.

Outline

- Letter opening (1–3)
- Thanksgiving and prayer (4–7)
- Paul's plea for Onesimus (8–21)
- Paul's personal request (22)
- Letter closing (23–25)

Interesting Features

- Paul makes heavy use of rhetoric (the art of persuasion) in this letter.
- Rather than call directly for the overthrow of the institution of slavery, Paul preaches a gospel of freedom and equality in Christ—a gospel that eventually destroys the institution.
- The important phrases "in Christ" (vv. 8, 20, 23) and "in the Lord" (vv. 16, 20) appear throughout the letter to illustrate the main theme.

Connections

This short letter serves as a powerful reminder that being "in Christ" changes how we should treat other people, especially people of different social, racial, and economic situations (Gal. 3:28). As brothers and sisters in Christ, we should respond differently to one another (e.g., forgiving, accepting, interceding, returning). The book of Philemon reminds us that a new relationship with God should result in new relationships with God's people.

Hebrews

"God Has Spoken to Us in His Son"

A double-edged sword

Central Teaching

Hebrews calls us to stay strong in the faith, fixing our eyes on Jesus, the supreme revelation of God to his people.

Memory Verses

> *Therefore, since we are surrounded by such a great cloud of witnesses, let us throw off everything that hinders and the sin that so easily entangles. And let us run with perseverance the race marked out for us, fixing our eyes on Jesus, the pioneer and perfecter of faith. (Heb. 12:1–2)*

Setting

No one is completely certain who wrote Hebrews (perhaps Paul, Barnabas, Luke, Apollos, Silvanus, or Philip?). Whereas Paul always identifies himself as the author, the writer of Hebrews does not identify himself. This author was neither an apostle nor an eyewitness of the life of Jesus (Heb. 2:3). He was, however, highly educated because of his polished Greek style, persuasive rhetorical arguments, and extensive knowledge of the Old Testament. He was also a powerful preacher and a committed follower of Jesus Christ. This description fits Apollos perhaps better than any of the others, but we must remain cautious.

The audience is likely a Christian house church or group of house churches somewhere near Rome. They were Christians with some previous connection to the Jewish synagogue and had faced opposition but not yet suffered martyrdom. Apparently one or more of these house churches began to pull away from the main body of believers in the city and was considering a return to Judaism in order to avoid more intense persecution (10:25). These discouraged believers were not growing spiritually and were in danger of drifting away from the true faith. It seems reasonable to date the letter in the mid-60s, at the beginning of Nero's persecution of the church in and around Rome.

Message

This letter is more specifically called a "word of exhortation" or a sermon (Heb. 13:22; cf.

A statue of an athlete tying a victor's ribbon around his head

A model of the tabernacle

Acts 13:15), and it challenges a group of fragile believers to persevere in their commitment to Christ rather than drift away in unbelief. God spoke supremely in Jesus Christ—the preexistent and sovereign Son, the only sufficient sacrifice, and the one who understands our weaknesses and speaks in our defense. Believers cannot ignore or dismiss Jesus if they want to stay properly related to God. To persuade his audience to persevere, the preacher combines words of warning (2:1–4; 3:7–19; 4:12–13; 6:4–8; 10:26–31; 12:25–29) with words of assurance (6:9–12, 19–20; 7:25; 10:14, 32–39). As a result, the book of Hebrews holds in tension the danger of failing to persevere in faith and God's promises for those who endure.

Outline

- Jesus, God's final Word (1:1–4)
- Jesus, provider of salvation, superior to the angels (1:5–2:18)
- Jesus's faithfulness calls us to faithfulness (3:1–4:13)
- The superiority of Jesus's priesthood and ministry (4:14–10:25)
- Call to persevere in the journey of faith (10:26–12:29)
- Practical exhortations (13:1–19)
- Closing (13:20–25)

Interesting Features

- Hebrews goes into great detail about Jewish worship practices, including the role of the high priest and the function of the tabernacle.
- Hebrews presents both the fear of God (warning) and the grace of God (comfort) as important spiritual realities that should not be neglected.
- In Hebrews we find a clear and strong emphasis on Jesus's full humanity and full deity.

Connections

Faith is easy until it's tested. The letter/sermon of Hebrews confronts a group of people who are thinking about giving up on the Christian faith. The author is a compassionate and capable preacher set on persuading and exhorting these believers with all his might in the hope of drawing them back to spiritual safety. In the darkest of times, we must fix our eyes on Jesus, the one who willingly endured this same darkness in order to reconcile us to the Father. He will never let us down.

James

True Faith Works

Central Teaching

Genuine faith will inevitably result in practical actions that honor God.

Memory Verses

> *Consider it pure joy, my brothers and sisters, whenever you face trials of many kinds, because you know that the testing of your faith produces perseverance. Let perseverance finish its work so that you may be mature and complete, not lacking anything. (James 1:2–4)*

Setting

The author identifies himself as "James, a servant of God and of the Lord Jesus Christ" (1:1). The best candidate is James, the half brother of Jesus and leader in the Jerusalem church. He became a believer after the resurrection of Jesus and was visited individually by the risen Lord (1 Cor. 15:7). According to early church history, James was stoned to death in AD 62 for his commitment to Christ. James writes to the "twelve tribes scattered among the nations" (1:1), most likely referring to Jewish Christians living outside Palestine. Some (or most) of these Christians may have come from the church in Jerusalem, which was scattered after the persecution associated with Stephen's death (Acts 8:1; 11:19). This letter must have been written prior to James's death in AD 62, and many scholars believe it to have been written in the late AD 40s, making it one of the earliest New Testament letters.

Message

James offers practical advice for living out the Christian faith in everyday life. He is extremely concerned with three key themes: trials and temptations, wisdom (especially as it relates to speech), and riches and poverty.

1. James urges his readers to "consider it pure joy" (1:2) when they encounter various kinds of trials, perhaps especially economic and social difficulties. They can respond with joy or deep contentment (in contrast to emotional happiness) because they know that God is using the trials to produce endurance and, over time, to make them mature and complete.
2. As Christians, we should ask God for wisdom when we need it, trusting in his

Ancient mirrors

An ancient decorated horse bit

kind and generous character; he will give it. True wisdom manifests itself in how we treat other believers and especially in how we use our speech. The key to godly wisdom has always been a healthy fear of or trust in the Lord.

3. Believers who find themselves in humble or humiliating financial circumstances can always put their confidence in their high standing with the Lord. The wealthy believer should remember the fleeting nature of his wealth and put his confidence in his relationship with God.

Outline

- Greetings (1:1)
- Three key themes (1:2–11)
- Three themes repeated (1:12–27)
- Three themes explained (2:1–5:18)
- Letter closing (5:19–20)

Interesting Features

- There are many parallels between James and the teachings of Jesus, especially the Sermon on the Mount (Matt. 5–7).
- The book of James was most likely written by the half brother of Jesus, who became a believer after Jesus's resurrection.
- Although James and Paul appear to contradict one another on the issue of faith and works (see James 2:24 and Gal. 2:15–16), further study reveals that they are addressing different issues.
- James is fond of commands. More than fifty commands can be found in the 108 verses of this letter.

Connections

Many of the trials mentioned by James were caused by rich, powerful people oppressing poor, vulnerable people. While condemning favoritism and calling for justice, James also encourages us to face trials with the right attitude—a peaceful confidence that God can use difficulty to make us more like Jesus. James calls us to reject worldly wisdom in favor of godly wisdom, especially in terms of the way that we speak. He also reminds us that biblical faith involves more than assenting to certain doctrines; genuine faith expresses itself in actions or deeds. One of the main ways that our faith should work is through using our possessions to meet the practical needs of others.

1 Peter

Stand Firm in the Face of Suffering

Roman woman with braided hair (likely Julia Domina, wife of Emperor Severus)

Central Teaching

God calls his persecuted people to stand firm in his grace, which allows believers to live godly lives in the midst of trials.

Memory Verse

> *And the God of all grace, who called you to his eternal glory in Christ, after you have suffered a little while, will himself restore you and make you strong, firm and steadfast. (1 Pet. 5:10)*

Setting

Both 1 and 2 Peter claim to have been written by Peter, an apostle of Jesus Christ (1 Pet. 1:1; 2 Pet. 1:1). In the first letter, Peter writes with the help of Silas (or Silvanus) as a fellow elder who has witnessed Christ's sufferings (5:1). Early Christian tradition unanimously supports Simon Peter as the author of 1 Peter.

Peter says he is writing from "Babylon"—most likely a veiled reference to Rome (1 Pet. 5:13)—to believers scattered in five Roman provinces of Asia Minor who are experiencing a degree of persecution for their faith. Church tradition reports that Peter was martyred sometime after Nero began persecuting Christians in AD 64. Therefore, 1 Peter was probably written around AD 63–64.

Message

When believers are threatened by persecution, the solution is to stand firm in the grace of God (5:12). Peter opens his letter by praising God for providing salvation through the death and resurrection of Jesus Christ. To live out this amazing salvation in the midst of suffering, believers need to prepare their minds for action, exercise self-control, fix their hope on what God has promised, resist conforming to the world, and live holy

Mount Hermon, the possible location of Jesus's transfiguration

Southwest corner of the Temple Mount

lives. Peter also affirms the importance of community to perseverance. When believers enter into a relationship with Jesus ("the living Stone"), they become "living stones" that are being built into a "spiritual house" (2:4–5). Composed of both Jews and Gentiles, the multicultural church is the people of God, a description once reserved only for Israel. Peter encourages his readers to embrace suffering in the name of the Lord by being prepared to respond properly to outsiders, following the example of Jesus, living urgently in light of Christ's return, and counting it a privilege to suffer. In his final exhortations (5:1–11), Peter addresses the elders or overseers who are charged with shepherding God's flock under their care.

Outline

- Greeting and praise to God for providing salvation (1:1–12)
- A call to holy living (1:13–2:3)
- A community belonging to God (2:4–10)
- Living godly lives among outsiders (2:11–3:12)
- Suffering unjustly for the name of the Lord (3:13–4:19)
- Final exhortations and closing (5:1–24)

Interesting Features

- First Peter speaks volumes about how Christians should understand and face suffering for the cause of Christ.
- One motivation for living godly lives in this world is the impact it will have on outsiders, which is an important topic in 1 Peter.
- First Peter 2 contains a fascinating metaphor for the church: living stones being built into a spiritual house or temple for God.
- Peter's first letter contains several powerful Christ-centered confessions (1:19–21; 2:21–25; 3:18–22).

Connections

Persecution takes various forms for Western Christians: ridicule, slander, ostracism, and economic discrimination (to name a few). First Peter provides much-needed perspective and encouragement for those who are suffering unjustly. We are reminded of who we are as God's people, the rock-solid nature of our hope in Christ, and the need to live holy lives. We should think about how best to respond to persecution, knowing that Jesus himself suffered and that suffering can lead to good. To face unjust suffering in a godly manner, we need a fresh reminder of God's grace, and that is just what 1 Peter provides.

2 Peter

Grow in the Knowledge of Christ

Central Teaching

Believers should grow in the grace and knowledge of Jesus Christ in order to stay true to the historic Christian faith and respond appropriately to false teaching.

Memory Verses

But do not forget this one thing, dear friends: With the Lord a day is like a thousand years, and a thousand years are like a day. The Lord is not slow in keeping his promise, as some understand slowness. Instead he is patient with you, not wanting anyone to perish, but everyone to come to repentance. (2 Pet. 3:8–9)

Setting

Both 1 and 2 Peter claim to have been written by the apostle Peter (1 Pet. 1:1; 2 Pet. 1:1). Because of stylistic differences between the two letters, the authorship of 2 Peter has been debated since ancient times. Yet the author claims to have been on the mount of transfiguration with Jesus (2 Pet. 1:16–18) and to have written a previous letter (3:1); what's more, he refers to Paul as "our dear brother" (3:15) and expects to die soon (1:14). Taken together, these claims point to the apostle Peter as the legitimate author of this letter.

Like Jude, 2 Peter was written as a response to the threat of false teaching. The primary heresy involved denying Christ's return and advocating immoral living and rejection of truth. Second Peter was written shortly before Peter's death, sometime between AD 64 and 68.

Message

Peter assures his readers that they have everything they need for life and godliness through their knowledge of God. Through God's calling and promises, believers can grow more like Christ, increasing in their knowledge of the Lord. Because Peter senses that his death is near, he feels a heavy responsibility to remind his readers of the basic truths of the faith—things they already know but need to live out consistently. He reminds them that Jesus will return, a reality the false teachers deny, and stresses that Jesus will return as Judge of those who deny God's truth and pervert the faith into an excuse for godless living. The Lord is faithful and will keep his promise to return. In the meantime,

God delays his judgment because he is patient, not wanting people to perish but desiring everyone to repent. When the day of the Lord does arrive, it will come suddenly and surprisingly, like a thief in the night (3:10). The present earth and heavens will be destroyed by fire, making way for the creation of the new heavens and the new earth.

Outline

- Greeting (1:1–2)
- Growing in our knowledge of God (1:3–11)
- Personal appeal (1:12–15)
- Reminder of the Lord's return (1:16–3:10)
- Closing remarks (3:11–18)

Interesting Features

- Peter reminds his readers that he personally witnessed Jesus's transfiguration, an event that previewed Jesus's final return in glory, which is a key theme of this letter.
- Peter refers to God's previous judgment of angels (2:4), which is perhaps a reference to the events mentioned in Genesis 6:1–4.
- Second Peter makes a strong statement concerning the divine inspiration of Scripture (1:20–21).
- Peter refers to the difficulty of understanding some of the apostle Paul's teachings (3:16).

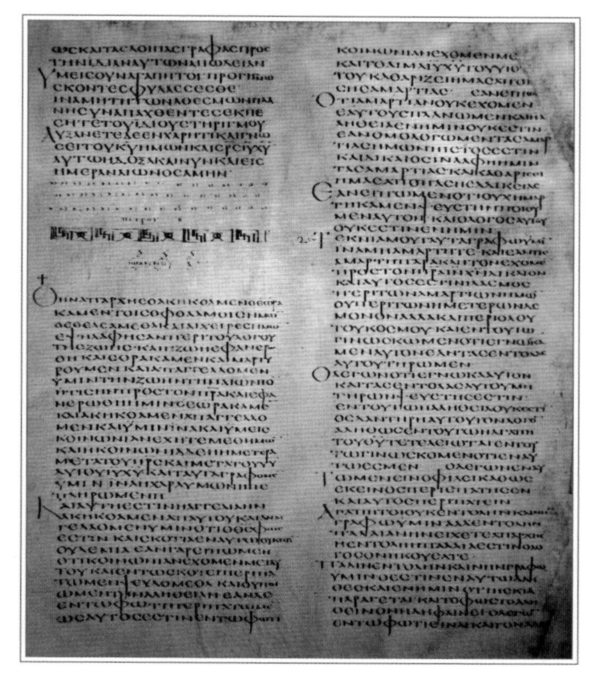

The end of 2 Peter and the beginning of 1 John in Codex Alexandrinus, an important early manuscript of the New Testament

Connections

Second Peter reminds us that knowledge is important in the Christian life. For instance, every few years some group sets a date when they claim Christ will return. Those who know the Scriptures won't be misled by such predictions because Jesus clearly taught that such speculation is not our responsibility. Second Peter specifically explains that Christ is delaying his return so that even more people may be brought to salvation. Believers should look forward to the day of the Lord and can even speed its coming (3:12). In the meantime, God's people should not be carried away by theological errors but should live godly lives so as to be found blameless when Christ comes.

1 John

True Christian Belief and Behavior

Central Teaching

The three marks of a true Christian are obedience to God, love for fellow believers, and a correct view of Jesus.

Memory Verse

> *If we confess our sins, he is faithful and just and will forgive us our sins and purify us from all unrighteousness. (1 John 1:9)*

Setting

Although the author never identifies himself, the traditional view is that John the apostle, the author of the Fourth Gospel, also wrote 1–3 John. Early church tradition indicates that John moved to Ephesus in the latter part of the first century to serve the churches in that region.

John is writing to Christians in and around Ephesus near the end of the first century (AD 70–90s). These churches were threatened by a false teaching that advocated knowledge rather than grace as the way to God and suggested that the human body was evil (an early form of gnosticism). Their emphasis on special *gnōsis* (Greek for knowledge) available only to insiders led to arrogance. Furthermore, their ideas about the body led some to treat their bodies harshly (asceticism) and others to indulge their bodily desires (immorality). For this reason, some denied Jesus's full humanity and deity. To complicate matters, those falling for this false teaching pulled away from the fellowship (1 John 2:19), claiming they had arrived at a state of sinless perfection (1 John 1:8, 10; 3:9–10).

Message

At a time when the traditional teaching about Jesus Christ and the Christian faith were being challenged, John offered a theological plumb line for his struggling churches. He writes to encourage the faithful by reminding them of what true Christians believe and how they should behave. The letter contains two purpose statements: to warn believers about the false teaching (2:26) and to help believers understand that they have eternal life (5:13).

John spent many years ministering in Ephesus. This tomb, within the remains of the Basilica of Saint John in Ephesus, is thought to be his burial site.

Ephesus was a thriving commercial, religious, and judicial center and the major city of Asia Minor. Here the theater of Ephesus can be seen rising behind the remains of the agora, the commercial center of the city.

John repeatedly emphasizes the marks of a true believer and how these counter the false teaching. True believers will walk in obedience rather than immorality (1:5–2:6; 2:28–3:10; 5:16–21). True believers will love one another rather than behave arrogantly (2:7–17; 3:11–24; 4:7–21). And true believers will possess an orthodox view of the full humanity and deity of Jesus Christ rather than promote a faulty view (2:18–27; 4:1–6; 5:1–15).

Outline

- Prologue (1:1–4)
- God is light—walk in the light (1:5–3:10)
- God is love—walk in love (3:11–5:12)
- Conclusion (5:13–21)

Interesting Features

- Of Jesus's twelve apostles, John probably lived the longest (until AD 98, according to the early church leader Irenaeus).
- There are many parallels between the Gospel of John and 1 John (e.g., eternal life, light, belief, Jesus as God's Son, the Holy Spirit, truth, abiding, new commandment of love).
- The term "antichrist" is only used four times in the Bible, all in the letters of John (1 John 2:18, 22; 4:3; 2 John 7).

Connections

The biblical view that Jesus is fully God and fully man rejects any teaching that denies his deity or humanity. In our contemporary pluralistic context, we need to guard our Christology. John also makes it clear that obedience to God is of utmost importance for the believer. Instead of excusing our sins or redefining sin, we must earnestly confess our sins to the Lord. When we do, we find he is faithful (willing) and just (able) to forgive us and cleanse us (1 John 1:9). Finally, John highlights the importance of love. We cannot claim to love God while we hate our fellow believers. Love and truth are friends rather than enemies. In our defense of truth, we must never lose love, and in our efforts to love, we must never neglect the truth.

2–3 John

2 John: Walk in Love and Truth
3 John: Imitate What Is Good

Central Teaching

Christians should use discernment with regard to Christian missionaries by lovingly supporting those who are genuinely sent by God.

Memory Verse

I have no greater joy than to hear that my children are walking in the truth. (3 John 4)

Setting

In both 2 and 3 John, the author describes himself as "the elder," a designation that also applies to the apostle John, who served as a respected leader in the early church. Early church traditions indicate that John moved to Ephesus in the latter part of the first century and served the churches in that region. Both letters were likely written from Ephesus about the same time as 1 John.

Second John is addressed to "the lady chosen by God and to her children" (v. 1), who could be either an individual Christian woman and her family or a figurative description of a local church. Because the "you" in 2 John 8, 10, and 12 is plural, because no family names are mentioned in 2 John 1 and 13, and because the "woman" is beloved by *all* who know the truth (v. 1), it seems that John is writing to a church. As for 3 John, the context seems to be a dispute between church members; an authoritarian leader in one of the churches has rejected traveling teachers sent out by John himself.

Message

In his first letter, John sets forth three marks of true Christianity: obedience to God, love for fellow believers, and a correct view of Jesus. These same truths are applied to specific situations in 2–3 John.

Second John may have been intended for a particular congregation. All three marks of the true believer are stressed again in 2 John, with special attention given to love and truth. John reminds the church of the love command they were given from the beginning and how love for one another is also connected to obedience to God. He insists that love and truth are not enemies but friends. John takes joy in the fact that his spiritual children are walking in truth even when tempted by false teachers, but he warns this congregation not to welcome the false teachers and give them a platform for their wicked work. He

Ancient Byzantine baptismal font at the Basilica of Saint John in Ephesus

This replica of a first-century house reminds us of how much John likes to compare the Christian community to a family and of the importance of hospitality.

instructs the church to use discernment in welcoming and supporting traveling teachers.

In his final letter John seeks to correct the problem of churches that reject traveling teachers sent out by the apostle himself. He urges believers to imitate what is good rather than what is evil and commends Gaius not only as an example of faithfulness to truth but also for showing hospitality to reliable traveling teachers. He rebukes Diotrephes for rejecting John's leadership and failing to show hospitality when needed.

Interesting Features

- Second John is the shortest book in the New Testament.
- When early Christians traveled, they relied on the hospitality of other believers for lodging and food. Third John speaks directly to the important practice of Christian hospitality.

Outline

- *2 John*
  - — Opening (1–3)
  - — Love (5–6)
  - — Truth (4, 7–11)
  - — Closing (12–13)
- *3 John*
  - — Opening (1)
  - — Commendation of Gaius (2–8)
  - — Rebuke for Diotrephes (9–11)
  - — Praise for Demetrius (12)
  - — Closing (13–14)

Connections

Taken together, 2 and 3 John offer a balanced approach to supporting Christian ministries. Second John teaches us to use discernment and good judgment. Before investing in a particular Christian ministry, we should investigate its message. Third John teaches us not to allow our love to grow cold toward all ministries just because some of them are misleading and deceptive. We should have discerning hearts to separate the true from the false and loving hearts to support in practical ways those involved in genuine Christian ministry.

Jude

Contend for the Faith

Central Teaching

In response to false teaching, God's people must be willing to contend for the faith that was once for all entrusted to the saints.

Memory Verses

> ***To him who is able to keep you from stumbling and to present you before his glorious presence without fault and with great joy—to the only God our Savior be glory, majesty, power and authority, through Jesus Christ our Lord, before all ages, now and forevermore! Amen. (Jude 24–25)***

Setting

The early church struggled with threats from both the outside (persecution) and the inside (false teaching). Jude was written in response to false teaching that was threatening the church from within (see Jude 4, 7–8, 10–12, 16–17, 19–20). The author describes himself as a "servant of Jesus Christ and a brother of James" (v. 1). Christian tradition identifies Jude as the half brother of Jesus (Matt. 13:55; Mark 6:3). His brother James wrote the New Testament letter of James.

Second Peter and Jude have a great deal in common, and one may have borrowed from the other. Most scholars assume that Jude was written prior to (but close to the same time as) 2 Peter, which was written shortly before Peter's death, sometime between AD 64 and 68. Jude was probably writing to a Jewish-Christian community outside of Palestine in a Gentile setting. The false teachers were probably Gentile since they were advocating such an immoral lifestyle.

Bronze coins depicting Nero and celebrating his military and civic achievements

Message

Jude warns of godless people who have infiltrated the church, advocating a false view of Jesus and twisting the grace of God into a license for godless living. He denounces these false teachers and warns of their impending judgment, calling them selfish shepherds because they live perverted lives, reject spiritual authority, and create chaos within the church. They are worldly people who do not have God's Spirit within them.

Jude then addresses the faithful about how to contend for the true faith. They need to grow in their knowledge of scriptural truth, pray in the Spirit, live in God's love, stay hopeful about Christ's return, and serve others.

Jude closes his short letter with a poetically powerful word of praise to God, who is able to protect his children and bring them into his glorious presence with great joy and without fault. The only God our Savior through Jesus Christ our Lord deserves all "glory, majesty, power and authority," from eternity past, to the present, and into eternity future (v. 25).

Outline

- Greeting (1–2)
- Occasion and purpose of the letter (3–4)
- Resisting false teachers (5–19)
- Contending for the faith (20–23)
- Doxology (24–25)

Interesting Features

- Jude is one of two letters in the New Testament that are believed to have been written by Jesus's half brothers (James and Jude). He was either the third or fourth son born to Joseph and Mary after Jesus (see Matt. 13:55; Mark 6:3).
- Jude quotes extrabiblical Jewish literature twice in his short letter: the *Testament of Moses* in verse 9 and *1 Enoch* in verses 14–15.
- Jude refers to angels several times in this short letter (vv. 6, 8–9, 14) and even names Michael the archangel (a rare event in Scripture).

Connections

Persecution takes various forms for Western Christians: ridicule, slander, ostracism, and economic discrimination, to name a few. And sometimes opposition occurs from within the church, from false teachers who have infiltrated the congregation. This is Jude's focus. Jude makes the point that false teachers sometimes need to be confronted as a matter of contending for the historic Christian faith. Not all conflict is unhealthy. In fact, conflict may be necessary when others are being steered away from the true gospel. Paul himself confronts false teachers in 2 Corinthians.

Sinai

Revelation

The Transforming Vision

A coin bearing the image of Emperor Domitian

Central Teaching

Revelation presents the final chapter in God's story of salvation: he defeats evil, reverses the curse of sin, restores creation, and lives forever among his people.

Memory Verse

> *They triumphed over him*
> *by the blood of the Lamb*
> *and by the word of their testimony;*
> *they did not love their lives so much*
> *as to shrink from death. (Rev. 12:11)*

Setting

The author of Revelation identifies himself as John, the servant of Jesus Christ (1:1, 4). There is some debate as to the identity of this John, but there is reliable evidence to conclude that this is the apostle John, who also wrote the Gospel of John. Banished to the island of Patmos for proclaiming the message about Jesus (1:9), John receives the heavenly vision that is Revelation on the Lord's day, or day of worship. His primary audience is the seven churches of Asia Minor mentioned in Revelation 2–3.

Revelation was written either shortly after the death of Nero (AD 68–69) or near the end of Domitian's reign (AD 95). Most scholars favor the later date, when persecution was threatening to spread across the Roman Empire. The imperial cult (i.e., the worship of the Roman emperor as Lord) was a powerful force because it united religious, political, social, and economic elements into a single force. The earliest and most basic Christian confession was "Jesus is Lord," and when Christians followed Jesus rather than Caesar, they were considered disloyal to the state and were subject to persecution. Some

Remains of the Temple of Flavian Sebastoi (emperors of the Flavian family) in Ephesus

Christians, however, chose to compromise their belief rather than stay faithful.

Message

Revelation addresses a situation in which pagan political power formed a partnership with false religion. Those who claimed to follow Christ faced mounting pressure to conform to this ungodly partnership at the expense of loyalty to Christ. The overall purpose of Revelation is to comfort those who are facing persecution and to warn those who are compromising by adhering to the world system.

To send this message, Revelation uses strange images and symbols as it combines the literary types of letter, prophecy, and apocalyptic. This picture language creates a symbolic world for the believers to enter as they hear the book. In doing so, they gain a heavenly perspective on current events; they see reality differently. While it may seem that Caesar is Lord, Revelation shows that God is in control of history and that Jesus is Lord. God will win in the end. As a result, believers are strongly encouraged to persevere in faithfulness to Jesus.

Outline

- Introduction and messages to the seven churches (1:1–3:22)
- Heavenly throne room vision (4:1–5:14)
- The seal judgments and first interlude (6:1–8:1)
- The trumpet judgments and second interlude (8:2–11:19)
- Third interlude: people of God vs. powers of evil (12:1–14:20)
- The bowl judgments (15:1–16:21)
- The destruction of "Babylon the Great" (17:1–19:5)
- The final victory and the new creation (19:6–22:5)
- Conclusion (22:6–21)

The "mountain of Megiddo" in Israel becomes a symbol for the final battle between God and the forces of evil (i.e., Armageddon in Rev. 16:12–16).

Interesting Features

- Revelation features three different literary types (genres): letter, prophecy, and apocalyptic. For this reason, it is a challenge to interpret.
- The book has much in common with Ezekiel, Daniel, and Zechariah, each of which contains similar prophetic-apocalyptic elements.
- Revelation alludes to the Old Testament more than any other New Testament book.

Connections

Revelation reminds us that God is sovereign and that Jesus is Lord. No matter how things appear in our nation or in our world, God is still on his throne. Our hope is that Jesus will return again to set things right. In the end, God wins! The book also tells us to expect opposition in this world. Even now, Christians throughout the world are being persecuted. We know that God will protect us spiritually, but we are not exempt from physical tribulation (cf. John 16:33). Revelation warns us against compromising our faith by adhering to the world system and calls us to overcome or endure in faithfulness to Jesus. Our present sufferings are not worth comparing to the glorious future God has in store for his people in the new creation.

The Parables of Jesus

Jesus was a master communicator, and one of his favorite tools of the trade was the parable. Approximately one-third of Jesus's teaching can be found in parables. Even people who are unfamiliar with the Bible have usually heard of the parable of the prodigal son or the parable of the good Samaritan. A parable (the term means "to throw alongside") is a short story with two levels of meaning in which certain details in the story represent something else. In the parable of the prodigal son, for example, the father represents God. In the story of the good Samaritan the priest and the Levite represent religious leaders who use their religious status as an excuse not to love others. Sometimes it is difficult to know how many details in these stories should stand for other things.

Jesus's parables typically make more than one point but should not be understood in a wildly allegorical fashion. A good rule of thumb is that there is one main point for each main character or set of characters.[1] All the other details are meant to enhance the story. The parable of the prodigal son in Luke 15:11–32 makes the following main points:

- Younger brother → Sinners may confess their sins and turn to God in repentance.
- Older brother → Those who claim to be God's people should not be resentful when God extends his grace to the undeserving; rather, they should rejoice.
- Forgiving father → God offers forgiveness to undeserving people.

Below Jesus's parables are divided up into one-point, two-point, and three-point parables.

One-Point Parables

- Mustard seed (Matt. 13:31–32; Mark 4:30–32; Luke 13:18–19)
- Leaven (Matt. 13:33; Luke 13:20–21)
- Hidden treasure (Matt. 13:44)
- Pearl of great price (Matt. 13:45–46)
- Tower builder (Luke 14:28–30)
- Warring king (Luke 14:31–33)

1. For this interpretive guideline, see the landmark work on Jesus's parables by Craig L. Blomberg, *Interpreting the Parables* (Downers Grove, IL: InterVarsity, 1990).

Two-Point Parables

- Secretly growing seed (Mark 4:26–29)
- Wise and foolish builders (Matt. 7:24–27; Luke 6:47–49)
- Householder and the thief (Matt. 24:42–44; Luke 12:35–40)
- Friend at midnight (Luke 11:5–8)
- Rich fool (Luke 12:16–21)
- Barren fig tree (Luke 13:6–9)
- Lowest seat at the feast (Luke 14:7–11)
- Unprofitable servant (Luke 17:7–10)
- Unjust judge (Luke 18:1–8)

Three-Point Parables

- Children in the marketplace (Matt. 11:16–19; Luke 7:31–35)
- Sower and the seed (Matt. 13:1–9, 18–23; Mark 4:1–9, 13–20; Luke 8:5–8, 11–15)
- Wheat and the tares (Matt. 13:24–30, 36–43)
- Dragnet (Matt. 13:47–50)
- Unforgiving servant (Matt. 18:23–35)
- Laborers in the vineyard (Matt. 20:1–16)
- Two sons (Matt. 21:28–32)
- Wicked tenants (Matt. 21:33–46; Mark 12:1–12; Luke 20:9–18)
- Wedding feast (Matt. 22:1–14)
- Faithful and unfaithful servants (Matt. 24:45–51; Luke 12:42–48)
- Ten maidens (Matt. 25:1–13)
- Talents (Matt. 25:14–30; Luke 19:12–27)
- Sheep and goats (Matt. 25:31–46)
- Two debtors (Luke 7:41–43)
- Good Samaritan (Luke 10:25–37)
- Great banquet (Luke 14:15–24)
- Lost sheep and lost coin (Luke 15:4–10)
- Lost (prodigal) son (Luke 15:11–32)
- Unjust steward (Luke 16:1–13)
- Rich man and Lazarus (Luke 16:19–31)
- Pharisee and the tax collector (Luke 18:9–14)

Through his parables, Jesus explains the true nature of the kingdom of God. Often, he begins a story with the words, "The kingdom of God is like . . ." (e.g., Matt. 13:44–45, 47; Mark 4:26; Luke 13:18). The kingdom of God is the central theme of Jesus's parables. Through these powerful stories we learn about who God is, what it means to live as a member of his kingdom community, and what happens if you choose to reject the King.

Jesus's parables provide some of the most fascinating and engaging reading in the entire Bible. He uses the stuff of ordinary life—family relationships, business practices, weddings, feasts, agriculture, politics—to teach us about God and his kingdom and how life should work in that kingdom. These stories are not incidental to the real teachings of Jesus. In many ways, the parables represent the very core of his teachings. As Jesus himself said, whoever has ears to hear had better listen.

The Miracles of Jesus

Jesus's miracles are very closely connected to his teaching about the kingdom of God, since they demonstrate that Jesus is indeed the Messiah and God's mighty power is at work through him. These mighty works provide glimpses of how life will go when God reigns over all.

The Gospels record roughly thirty-five miracles of Jesus, which fall into four different categories: healings, resuscitations, exorcisms, and nature miracles.

The healing miracles clearly show the kingdom of God breaking into this world. In Matthew 11, John the Baptist (who is in prison) sends disciples to ask Jesus if he is the "Coming One" (Messiah). Jesus responds by saying, "Go back and report to John what you hear and see: The blind receive sight, the lame walk, those who have leprosy are cleansed, the deaf hear, the dead are raised, and the good news is proclaimed to the poor" (Matt. 11:4–5). In other words, the healing miracles are evidence that the kingdom has arrived.

Healing Miracles

Man with leprosy	Matt. 8:1–4; Mark 1:40–45; Luke 5:12–15
Centurion's servant	Matt. 8:5–13; Luke 7:1–10
Healing Peter's mother-in-law	Matt. 8:14–17; Mark 1:29–31; Luke 4:38–39
Paralyzed man	Matt. 9:1–8; Mark 2:1–12; Luke 5:17–26
Bleeding woman	Matt. 9:20–22; Mark 5:25–29; Luke 8:43–48
Two blind men	Matt. 9:27–31
Man with withered hand	Matt. 12:9–14; Mark 3:1–6; Luke 6:6–11
Blind Bartimaeus	Matt. 20:29–34; Mark 10:46–52; Luke 18:35–43
Deaf and mute man	Mark 7:31–37
Blind man	Mark 8:22–26
Woman crippled for eighteen years	Luke 13:10–17
Man with dropsy	Luke 14:1–6
Ten men with leprosy	Luke 17:11–19
High priest's servant	Luke 22:49–51; John 18:10–11
Royal official's son at Cana	John 4:46–54
Paralytic at Bethesda	John 5:1–18
Man born blind	John 9:1–41

On three occasions, Jesus raises people from the dead. He resuscitates or revives the people to normal mortal life, eventually to die again. Resurrection occurs at the end of this present age when Christians receive new bodies (see 1 Cor. 15). The message is the same as with the healing miracles, only more dramatic—the kingdom of God is a kingdom of life! One day death will be defeated and completely eliminated from God's new creation.

Resuscitation Miracles

Jairus's daughter	Matt. 9:18–26; Mark 5:22–24, 35–43; Luke 8:41–42, 49–56
Widow's son at Nain	Luke 7:11–16
Lazarus	John 11:1–45

By casting out demons, Jesus launches an all-out, frontal assault on the kingdom of Satan by the power of the kingdom of God. In an exorcism, Jesus attacks Satan and takes back a precious life that has been held captive and tortured by the enemy. These liberated captives begin to be human once again.

Exorcism Miracles

Possessed man in synagogue	Mark 1:23–27; Luke 4:33–36
Gadarene demoniac(s)	Matt. 8:28–34; Mark 5:1–20; Luke 8:26–39
Daughter of Canaanite woman	Matt. 15:21–28; Mark 7:24–30
Demon-possessed boy	Matt. 17:14–20; Mark 9:14–29; Luke 9:37–43
Blind, mute possessed man	Matt. 12:22; Luke 11:14
Mute possessed man	Matt. 9:32–34

The nature miracles often carry a great deal of symbolic significance. For example, the feeding of the multitudes teaches that God supplies what we need for life (i.e., Jesus as the bread of life). Turning water into wine symbolizes how the "new wine" of the kingdom is replacing the "water" of legalistic Judaism. The cursing of the fig tree shows what God will do with Israel if it fails to respond to Jesus and the kingdom he inaugurates. The nature miracles also show that God is renewing the whole created order.

Nature Miracles

Calming the storm	Matt. 8:23–27; Mark 4:35–41; Luke 8:22–25
Feeding of five thousand	Matt. 14:15–21; Mark 6:35–44; Luke 9:12–17; John 6:5–15
Walking on water	Matt. 14:22–33; Mark 6:45–52; John 6:16–21
Feeding of four thousand	Matt. 15:32–39; Mark 8:1–9
Coin in fish's mouth	Matt. 17:24–27
Withering of the fig tree	Matt. 21:18–22; Mark 11:12–14, 20–25
First catch of fish	Luke 5:1–11
Turning water into wine	John 2:1–11
Second catch of fish	John 21:1–14

At the very beginning of this book we talked about living the story. One way we can live the story is by taking a fresh look at Jesus's miracles. However, we should never demand that God work a miracle so that we will believe in him. Faith sometimes stands out as the reason that Jesus works a miracle (though not always), but Jesus's many miracles did not always produce faith in those who witnessed them (e.g., even the raising of Lazarus in John 11 produces mixed results). To demand miracles from God is to fall victim to one of the temptations Jesus faced in the wilderness—testing God rather than trusting him. That being said, many of us struggle with an opposite problem. Having been unduly influenced by a naturalistic worldview, we struggle to open ourselves to God's special activity in our lives and our churches. Have we withdrawn from the mystery of the miraculous into the comfortable confines of materialism and rationalism?

Jesus should be our focus, not miracles. But the Spirit of Jesus continues to work miracles today, and we should be open to them. Above all, Jesus's miracles should encourage us as visible reminders of the way things ought to be and one day will be when the kingdom of God comes in all its fullness.

Dictionary of People in the Old Testament

Aaron The older brother and close associate of Moses, who was appointed by God to be the first high priest of Israel. See Exodus–Deuteronomy.

Abigail A wise and discerning woman, she was originally the wife of Nabal, a foolish but wealthy man whom God struck dead for dishonoring David. She became the wife of David after Nabal's death. See 1 Samuel 25.

Abimelek Means "my father is king." Five people in the Old Testament have this name: (1) the king of Gerar who was deceived by Abraham regarding Sarah, Abraham's wife (see Gen. 20:1–18; 21:22–24); (2) the king's descendant, also king of Gerar (see Gen. 26:1–35); (3) the ruler who succeeded his father Gideon by murdering his seventy brothers (see Judg. 9); (4) the priest in the time of David (see 1 Chron. 18:16 NASB and NIVmg); and (5) a generic reference to Philistine king Achish (see the attribution of Ps. 34 and 1 Sam. 21:10–15).

Abram/Abraham Called by God to be the father/founder of the Israelite nation and the recipient of a central covenant with God. See Genesis 12–25.

Absalom Third son of King David. He tried to overthrow his father and was killed by David's commander, Joab. See 2 Samuel 13–19.

Adam The first created person. See Genesis 1–5.

Ahab Evil king of Israel (871–852 BC) and opponent of the prophet Elijah. See 1 Kings 16–22.

Amos Earliest of the writing prophets. In the eighth century BC he preached judgment against Israel for idolatry and injustices. See the book of Amos.

Asaph A priest and musician who led worship in the time of King David. See 1 Chronicles 15–16; 25; 2 Chronicles 5:11–14; and Psalms 50; 73–83.

Bathsheba Beautiful woman with whom King David had a scandalous affair. She later married David and became the mother of Solomon. See 2 Samuel 11–12 and 1 Kings 1.

Benjamin Youngest son of Jacob and Rachel. The father of the tribe of Benjamin. See Genesis 35:24; 42:1–16; and Exodus 1:3.

Boaz Ancestor of David. Wealthy Bethlehem landowner who married Ruth the Moabite. See Ruth 2–4.

Caleb One of the two (out of twelve) spies who trusted God and urged the Israelites to conquer the promised land of Canaan. He later played an important role in conquering the land. See Numbers 13–14 and Joshua 14–15.

Cyrus King of Persia (559–530 BC) who conquered Babylon in 539 BC and decreed that the exiled Israelites in Babylonia could return to their home country. See 2 Chronicles 36:22–23; Ezra 1–6; and Isaiah 44:28–45:3.

Darius I King of Persia (521–486 BC) during the time that the returned exiles rebuilt the temple. See Ezra 4–6; Haggai; and Zechariah 1–8.

Darius the Mede Probably another name for Gubaru, a general under King Cyrus who captured Babylon and ruled as a governor for Cyrus. See Daniel 5:30–6:28.

David Second King of Israel (1010–970 BC). He established Jerusalem as the capital and worship center of Israel. Many of the psalms are attributed to him. God promised that one of his descendants would be the messianic king. See 1 Samuel 16–2 Samuel 24; 1 Kings 1–2; and 1 Chronicles 10–29.

Deborah One of the strong rulers (judges) of Israel who led the nation to victory over the Canaanites. See Judges 4–5.

Ehud One of the rulers (judges) of Israel. He freed the Israelites from Moabite domination by assassinating the Moabite king. See Judges 3:12–30.

Elijah A powerful and true prophet of God in the ninth century BC. He opposed the wicked rulers Ahab and Jezebel, defeating and killing many of the prophets of Baal at Mount Carmel. See 1 Kings 17–2 Kings 2.

Elisha True prophet and successor of Elijah. He opposed the worship of the false god Baal and demonstrated the power of God through numerous miracles. See 1 Kings 19 and 2 Kings 2–13.

Ephraim Second son of Joseph and father of the tribe of Ephraim, one of the largest and most influential of the ten northern tribes of Israel. See Genesis 41:52; 48:1–20; and Hosea 4–14.

Esther Beautiful Jewish woman living in exile in Persia who became queen and used her influence to prevent the Jews from being destroyed. See the book of Esther.

Eve The first created woman. Her name means "living one" or "life giver." See Genesis 2–4.

Ezekiel Priest taken into exile by the Babylonians in 598 BC. He prophesied to the exiles about disobedience, the sovereignty and presence of God, and the new temple. See the book of Ezekiel.

Ezra Priest and scribe during the postexilic period. In 458 BC he returned to Judah and worked to reestablish the proper worship of God among the Jews who had returned from exile. See Ezra 7–10 and Nehemiah 8:1–18; 12:36.

Gideon Israelite leader (judge) who miraculously delivered the Israelites from the Midianites. See Judges 6:1–8:35.

Habakkuk Literary prophet in Judah from the late seventh century BC. See the book of Habakkuk.

Haggai Literary prophet in Judah after the exile (520 BC) who exhorted the returned exiles to rebuild the temple. See the book of Haggai.

Hezekiah King in Judah (727–698 BC) and contemporary of the prophet Isaiah. He tried to return Judah to a true worship of God. See 2 Kings 18–20; 2 Chronicles 29–32; and Isaiah 36–39.

Hosea Literary prophet (about 760–720 BC) who, at God's direction, married a harlot to illustrate God's relationship with Israel. See the book of Hosea.

Isaac Patriarch of Israel, son of Abraham, husband to Rebekah, and father of Jacob.

See Genesis 17:19–21; 21:1–28:15; and 35:27–29.

Isaiah Late eighth-century BC literary prophet in Jerusalem during the reigns of Jotham, Ahaz, and Hezekiah. He preached judgment for idolatry and injustice but also messianic restoration. See 2 Kings 19–20; 2 Chronicles 26:22; 32:20, 32; and the book of Isaiah.

Jacob Son of Isaac, brother of Esau, husband of Leah and Rachel, and father to twelve sons. God renamed him "Israel," and his sons became the tribes of Israel. See Genesis 25; 27–35; 37; and 46–49.

Jephthah Leader (judge) of Israel who sacrificed his daughter because of a rash and foolish vow. See Judges 11:1–12:7.

Jeremiah Major literary prophet in Jerusalem (626–586 BC). He warned Judah of the coming Babylonian invasion, experienced personal persecution, wrote numerous laments, and prophesied concerning the new covenant. See 2 Chronicles 35:25; 36:12–22; Ezra 1:1; the book of Jeremiah; and Daniel 9:2.

Jezebel Sidonian (Canaanite), Baal-worshiping queen and wife of King Ahab of Israel. She persecuted the prophet Elijah. See 1 Kings 16:29–33; 18:4–21:26; and 2 Kings 9.

Job A wealthy man from Uz (Edom) who challenged God's justice when he experienced tragedy. He was later restored by God. See the book of Job.

Joel Literary prophet known for visions of locust plagues (judgment) and the promise of the Holy Spirit coming on all of God's people. See the book of Joel.

Jonah Reluctant prophet swallowed by a huge fish for disobeying God. He later preached to the people of Nineveh, who listened and repented. See 2 Kings 14:25 and the book of Jonah.

Jonathan Eldest son of King Saul and close friend of David. See 1 Samuel 13–14; 18–20; and 2 Samuel 1.

Joshua Aide and successor of Moses. He led the Israelites into the promised land of Canaan. See Exodus 17; Numbers 11:28; 13:16; 14:6–38; and the book of Joshua.

Josiah King of Judah (640–609 BC) who tried (unsuccessfully) to turn the people away from idolatry and back to faithful worship of God. See 2 Kings 22–23; 2 Chronicles 34–35; and Jeremiah 1:2–3.

Levi Son of Jacob and founding father of the tribe of Levi, the tribe God chose to serve as priests. See Genesis 29:34; 34:25–30; Exodus 32:26–28; and Numbers 1:47–53.

Lot Nephew and companion of Abraham. He separated from his uncle to live in the city of Sodom and was later rescued by angels. See Genesis 11:27–14:16 and 18:16–19:38.

Malachi The last of the literary prophets (about 430 BC), known for prophesying Elijah's return (which was fulfilled by John the Baptist). See the book of Malachi.

Micah May refer to (1) a disobedient Levite who became a priest of Dan and worshiped idols (see Judges 17–18) or (2) a literary Israelite prophet of the late eighth century BC who preached repentance, judgment, and restoration (see Jeremiah 26:18 and the book of Micah).

Miriam Sister of Moses and Aaron. She protected Moses and helped lead the Israelites out of Egypt. See Exodus 2:4–10; 15:20–21; Numbers 12:1–15; and Micah 6:4.

Moses Chosen by God to lead the Israelites out of Egypt and into covenant relationship with God at Mount Sinai. See Exodus–Deuteronomy.

Naaman Syrian general healed of leprosy by following the prophet Elisha's directions. See 2 Kings 5.

Nehemiah Hebrew administrator in the Persian court who returned to Jerusalem in 445 BC to help the inhabitants rebuild the walls and the nation. See the book of Nehemiah.

Obadiah Means "servant of the Lord" and refers to thirteen different people in the Old Testament. Two of the most famous of these are (1) the literary prophet who preached judgment on Edom (see the book of Obadiah) and (2) the palace administrator for King Ahab who secretly hid one hundred true prophets from Queen Jezebel during the time of Elijah (see 1 Kings 18).

Rebekah One of the matriarchs, wife of Isaac, and mother of Jacob and Esau. See Genesis 24–28.

Ruth Moabite woman who faithfully followed her mother-in-law to Israel, met and married Boaz, and became an ancestor of David. See the book of Ruth.

Samson Self-centered leader (judge) of Israel who used great strength to fight the Philistines. See Judges 13–16.

Samuel Judge, priest, and prophet who oversaw the transition from the time of the judges to the monarchy. He anointed King Saul and then King David. See 1 Samuel 1–19; 25:1; and 28:3–25.

Sarai/Sarah One of the matriarchs, wife of Abraham and mother of Isaac. See Genesis 11:29–13:1; 16:1–21:12; and 23:1–19.

Saul First King of Israel. He squandered the opportunities of his reign through disobedience to God and was replaced by David. See 1 Samuel 9–31 and 1 Chronicles 10.

Solomon Son of David and Bathsheba, opulent king of Israel (971–931 BC). He constructed a beautiful temple for God but engaged in idolatry and forced labor. See 1 Kings 1–11; 1 Chronicles 22; 29; and 2 Chronicles 1–9.

Zechariah Means "the Lord remembers" and refers to twenty-six different people in the Old Testament. The most famous Zechariah was a literary postexilic prophet (520–518 BC) who encouraged the returned exiles to rebuild the temple and to anticipate the coming Messiah. See the book of Zechariah.

Zephaniah Refers to four people in the Old Testament. The most famous Zephaniah was a literary prophet in the time of King Josiah (640–609 BC). See the book of Zephaniah.

Zerubbabel Jewish leader and Persian-appointed governor of Judah (538–515 BC) who helped lead the Jewish exiles back to Jerusalem to reestablish the nation. See Ezra 2–5; Nehemiah 12; Haggai 1–2; and Zechariah 4.

Dictionary of People in the New Testament

Andrew One of Jesus's twelve apostles and brother of Simon Peter. See Matthew 4:18; 10:2; Mark 1:16, 29; John 1:40–44; 12:22; and Acts 1:13.

Anna An elderly Jewish prophetess who worshiped daily in the Jerusalem temple and was present at the dedication of the baby Jesus. See Luke 2:36–38.

Apollos An Alexandrian Jewish Christian with profound knowledge of the Old Testament and powerful rhetorical skills. He was instructed in the Christian faith by Priscilla and Aquila and ministered alongside Paul in Corinth. See Acts 18:18–19:1; 1 Corinthians 1:12; 3:4–22; 4:6; 16:12; and Titus 3:13.

Aquila A Jewish-Christian leatherworker from Pontus, husband of Priscilla and coworker of Paul in cities such as Corinth, Ephesus, and Rome. See Acts 18; Romans 16:3; 1 Corinthians 16:19; and 2 Timothy 4:19.

Barnabas (also called Joseph, the Levite) Missionary companion of Paul and cousin of John Mark. His name (in Aramaic) means "son of encouragement," and he was known for his compassionate heart and commitment to reconciliation. See Acts 4:36; 9:27; 11:22–15:39; 1 Corinthians 9:6; Galatians 2; and Colossians 4:10.

Caesar Augustus Title given to the Roman emperor Octavian (31 BC–AD 14), who ruled the Roman Empire when Jesus was born. See Luke 2:1.

Caiaphas High priest (AD 18–36) and the son-in-law of Annas, the former high priest. He is best known for interrogating Jesus and handing him over to Pilate. See Matthew 26:3, 57; Luke 3:2; John 11:49; 18:13–28; and Acts 4:6.

Cornelius A Roman centurion who lived in Caesarea Maritima. A God-fearing man, he received a vision from the Lord to bring Peter to Caesarea to preach the good news. See Acts 10.

Felix The Roman governor of Judea when Paul was arrested in Jerusalem. He heard Paul's case in Caesarea, but because of his greed and desire to please the Jews, he left Paul in prison two more years until Festus took over. See Acts 23–25.

Festus The governor of Judea (AD 59–62) who succeeded Felix. When he heard Paul's case and Paul appealed to Caesar, he granted his request. See Acts 25–26.

Herod Agrippa I Grandson of Herod the Great, known for persecuting the early church (he imprisoned Peter and killed James, the brother of John). Luke attributes his sudden death to the judgment of God. See Acts 12.

Herod Antipas One of the sons of Herod the Great. He ruled as a tetrarch of Galilee and Perea, had John the Baptist imprisoned and beheaded, and interviewed Jesus prior to his crucifixion. See Matthew 14 and Luke 3; 23.

Herod the Great Known as King Herod, he ruled Palestine (37–4 BC) and was known for being a skilled politician and ambitious builder (expanded the Jerusalem temple). He ordered the male infants of Bethlehem to be killed around the time of Jesus's birth. See Matthew 2.

James, brother of Jesus Prominent leader in the Jerusalem church after Jesus's resurrection. He later worked with Paul at the Jerusalem Council and is the likely author of the Letter of James. See Acts 15 and James.

James, the disciple Son of Zebedee, older brother of John, and one of the twelve apostles of Jesus. He was killed by Herod Agrippa I in AD 40. See Matthew 4:21; Mark 1:19, 29; 3:17–18; 10:35–41; and Acts 12:2.

John, the apostle The son of Zebedee, younger brother of James and (along with Peter and James) part of Jesus's inner circle of disciples (he was also known as the disciple "whom Jesus loved" [John 13:23]). Likely wrote the Gospel of John and possibly 1–3 John and Revelation. See Matthew–Acts.

John the Baptist (or Baptizer) A Jewish prophet, born to Zechariah and Elizabeth, who prepared the way for Jesus the Messiah by preaching repentance and performing baptisms. John was imprisoned and killed by Herod Antipas. See Matthew 3; 11:1–18; 14:1–12; Mark 1:1–15; 6:14–29; Luke 1; 3:1–20; 7:18–35; 9:1–20; and John 1; 3:22–36; 10:40–41.

Joseph A descendant of King David and the husband of Mary, the mother of Jesus. Served as father for Jesus and probably died before Jesus's earthly ministry began. See Matthew 1–2 and Luke 1–2.

Joseph of Arimathea A member of the Jewish Sanhedrin and a secret follower of Jesus. He asked Pilate for Jesus's body and buried Jesus in his own tomb. See John 19:38.

Judas One of the twelve apostles chosen by Jesus. He later betrayed Jesus. See Matthew 10:4; 26:14–16, 20–30, 47–50; 27:3–5; Mark 3:19; 14:10–11, 18–21, 43–46; Luke 6:16; 22:3–6, 21–23, 47–48; John 6:71; 12:4–6; 13:2, 18–30; 18:2–5; and Acts 1:16–18.

Jude (also called Judas) The brother of James, half brother of Jesus, and author of the Letter of Jude. See Matthew 13; Mark 6; and Jude.

Lazarus The brother of Mary and Martha of Bethany. Famously raised from the dead by Jesus. See John 11–12.

Luke Gentile physician, missionary companion of Paul, and author of Luke-Acts (more than one-fourth of the New Testament). He was a careful historian and theologian as well as a faithful coworker. See Colossians 4:14; 2 Timothy 4:11; and Philemon 1:24.

Mark, John A Jewish Christian from Jerusalem, cousin to Barnabas, and the likely author of the Gospel of Mark (following Peter's teaching). He abandoned Paul's missionary team on their first journey but was later reconciled with the apostle. See Acts 12:12–25; 15:37–39; Colossians 4:10; 2 Timothy 4:11; and 1 Peter 5:13.

Martha Sister of Mary and Lazarus from Bethany. Best known for her preoccupation with serving her guests while her sister Mary listened to Jesus (see Luke 10:38–42). She boldly confessed Jesus as "the Messiah, the Son of God" (John 11:27).

Mary, friend of Jesus Sister of Martha and Lazarus from Bethany. Jesus commends her for listening to him and for anointing his body for burial with expensive perfume. See Luke 10:38–42 and John 11:1–12:11.

Mary, mother of Jesus Young girl from Galilee who became pregnant by the Holy Spirit while still a virgin. She gave birth to Jesus and was known for her humble obedience to God's unique calling on her life. While on the cross, Jesus entrusts Mary to John's care. See Matthew 1; Luke 1–2; and John 2:1–12; 19:25–27.

Mary Magdalene A faithful follower of Jesus, who cured her of evil spirits and diseases. She was the first to witness the empty tomb and the resurrected Jesus. See Luke 8:1–3 and John 20:1–18.

Matthew (Levi) One of the twelve apostles and the traditional author of the Gospel of Matthew. Before following Jesus, Matthew worked as a tax collector for Herod Antipas. Mark and Luke refer to him as Levi. See Matthew 9:9–13; Mark 2:14; and Luke 5:27.

Nathanael Disciple of Jesus (probably also known as Bartholomew) whose initial skepticism turned to faith after Jesus called him. He was one of the first to see the risen Christ. See John 1:45–49; 21:2.

Nicodemus A Pharisee and a member of the Jewish Sanhedrin who came at night for a discussion with Jesus about being born again. After Jesus's death, he helped Joseph of Arimathea bury Jesus. See John 3:1–21; 19:39.

Paul A Jewish Christian (formerly a Pharisee and student of Gamaliel) who was dramatically converted and commissioned by Jesus to preach the gospel to the Gentiles. He took several missionary journeys, worked with numerous other believers, and wrote many New Testament letters. Also known as Saul. See Acts 13–28; Romans–Philemon; and 2 Peter 3:15.

Peter (also Simon Peter or Cephas) Brother of Andrew, a member of Jesus's inner circle, and the chief spokesman for the disciples. He confessed Jesus as the Christ but later denied him three times. He went on to preach Christ powerfully at Pentecost and beyond and to write 1–2 Peter. Tradition maintains that Peter was martyred by Nero around AD 64. See Matthew–Acts; Galatians 1:18–2:14; and 1–2 Peter.

Philemon The leader of a house church in Colossae who received a letter from Paul asking him to take back his runaway slave Onesimus without punishing him. See Philemon.

Philip, the apostle One of Jesus's twelve apostles. He was from Bethsaida (like Andrew and Peter) and introduced Nathanael to Jesus. See Matthew 10:3; Mark 3:18; Luke 6:14; and John 1:43–51; 6:1–15; 12:20–36; 14:5–14.

Philip, the evangelist Chosen by the Jerusalem church as one of seven men tasked with distributing food to its widows. Became a bold evangelist to the city of Samaria, surrounding towns, and even an Ethiopian eunuch. See Acts 8.

Pilate, Pontius Roman governor of Judea who presided over Jesus's trial and authorized his crucifixion under pressure from the Jewish leaders. See Matthew 27; Mark 15; Luke 23; and John 18:28–19:42.

Priscilla (or Prisca) Wife of Aquila and coworker of the apostle Paul. She is often listed first when the pair is mentioned, probably highlighting her social status or prominence in the Christian community. See Acts 18; Romans 16:3; 1 Corinthians 16:19; and 2 Timothy 4:19.

Silas Jewish Christian who served as a leader of the Jerusalem church. He took the letter related to the Jerusalem Council to Antioch and served as a missionary coworker of Paul. He also played an important role in writing several New Testament letters. See Acts 15–18; 2 Corinthians 1:19; 1 Thessalonians 1:1; 2 Thessalonians 1:1; and 1 Peter 5:12.

Simeon A righteous man in Jerusalem who received a vision that he would see the Messiah. After seeing Jesus, he offered a prayer of praise and prophesied about Jesus's role as it related to Israel. See Luke 2:25–34.

Stephen Chosen by the Jerusalem church as one of seven men tasked with distributing food to its widows. This man "full of faith and of the Holy Spirit" (Acts 6:5) became the first known Christian martyr, being stoned to death by the Jewish Sanhedrin. See Acts 6–8.

Thomas One of Jesus's twelve disciples, also known as "Didymus" (the twin). He refused to believe Jesus's resurrection ("doubting Thomas") until Jesus appeared to him; Thomas then confessed him as his Lord and God. See Matthew 10:3; Mark 3:18; Luke 6:15; and John 11:16; 14:5; 20:24–28; 21:2.

Timothy One of Paul's most trusted coworkers. He became a believer during Paul's first missionary journey and accompanied Paul for much of the rest of his ministry. He is listed as cosender in many of Paul's Letters and served faithfully in numerous places. Paul refers to Timothy as "my dear son" (2 Tim. 1:2) and sent him two letters (1–2 Tim.) near the end of his life. See Acts 16–20; Romans 16:21; 1 Corinthians 4:17; 16:10; 2 Corinthians 1; Philippians 1–2; Colossians 1:1; 1 Thessalonians 1–3; 2 Thessalonians 1:1; and 1–2 Timothy.

Titus A Gentile Christian and Paul's trusted coworker. He was responsible for the collection gathered for the Jerusalem church, carried Paul's letter (2 Corinthians) to that difficult church, and ministered in tough places (e.g., Crete). See 2 Corinthians 2:13; 7:6–8:23; 12:18; Galatians 2:1–3; 2 Timothy 4:10; and Titus 1:4.

Image Credits

Additional Image Credits

Photos on pages 28, 34, 38, 40 (both images), 44, 46 (bottom), 48 (bottom), 50 (bottom), 52 (top), 54 (both images), 56 (bottom), 58 (bottom), 59, 60, 61 (bottom), 66, 133 are copyright © Baker Publishing Group and Dr. James C. Martin. Courtesy of the British Museum, London, England.

Photo on page 29 is copyright © Baker Publishing Group and Dr. James C. Martin. Collection of the Israel Museum, Jerusalem, and courtesy of the Israel Antiquities Authority, exhibited at the Israel Museum, Jerusalem.

Photos on pages 27, 46 (top), 64, 134 are copyright © Baker Publishing Group and Dr. James C. Martin. Courtesy of Musée du Louvre; Autorisation de photographer et de filmer—LOUVRE, Paris, France.

Photos on pages 42, 57 are copyright © Baker Publishing Group and Dr. James C. Martin. Courtesy of the Archaeological Museum of Istanbul, Turkish Ministry of Antiquities.

Photo on page 62 is copyright © Baker Publishing Group and Dr. James C. Martin. Courtesy of the Oriental Institute of the University of Chicago.

Photo on page 51 is copyright © Direct Design.

Photo on page 36 is copyright © John A. Beck.

Photo on page 130 is copyright © Nevit Dilmen/ Wikimedia.